Even As Your Soul Prospers

Realize Your Purpose, Release Your Blessings

EVEN AS YOUR SOUL PROSPERS

Realize Your Purpose, Release Your Blessings

by

Thomas Weeks, III

Harrison House
Tulsa, Oklahoma

Edit originally developed by Paula Bryant, ASarah Publications C • E • S

08 07 06 05 04   10 9 8 7 6 5 4 3 2 1

Even As Your Soul Prospers:
Realize Your Purpose, Release Your Blessings
ISBN 1-57794-710-X
Copyright © 2004 by Thomas Weeks, III
Thomas Weeks, III Ministries
P.O. Box 60866
Washington, DC 20039

Published by Harrison House, Inc.
P.O. Box 35035
Tulsa, Oklahoma 74153

Acknowledgments

The legacy continues. This book celebrates the life of my grandfather, Bishop Thomas John Weeks, Sr., the patriarch of our family who brought ministry from the British West Indies all the way to Boston, Massachusetts.

Papa (as we call you), you are a shining example of soul prosperity. Even at the age of eighty-six, you've continued to birth and pioneer churches around the world. This book represents your legacy of prayers, love, support, and wisdom that you've passed on to my father, and through him, to me. May this work be a landmark of our family legacy in the earth. I love you, Papa.

Contents

FOREWORD

By Dr. Juanita Bynum Weeks

During the last several years, I have observed as God has been preparing the body of Christ for the end time revival. And I have watched as the Scriptures foretelling the events of the end times have begun being fulfilled according to the Lord's timing. During this time, the Spirit of the Lord has repeatedly led me to read the book of Revelation—and particularly the third chapter about the seven churches. When He began to show me the seven stages of the church, one stood out in my spirit more than the others (not that the others aren't just as important, but I believe that God will magnify a segment of His Word to address what is pertinent in that particular season).

I immediately began to receive the Word of the Lord for myself (as the first partaker of the message) concerning the church that stood out to me, the Church of Laodicea. After taking that word before Him in prayer, the message that came through to my spirit wouldn't leave me! I couldn't shake it. So I hid that word in my heart, because I knew God was waiting for a specific time for me to deliver it.

A few years ago, I underwent surgery and recuperated at home for two months. As I sat and watched several Christian channels, it seemed as though every program was on prosperity! I didn't understand at first why I was bothered after about the fifth or sixth week of watching the programs. Then the Spirit of the Lord began to speak. He revealed to me that He was requiring me, as a prophet, to begin preaching balance to the nature of the message of prosperity that had become prevalent in recent years. He was charging me to bring people to clarity, to bring people back to the true Source of not only prosperity, but of all things good. We can give all the financial seeds we want and expect a financial return, but true prosperity can only be obtained when our inner man, *our soul,* begins to line up with the Word of God.

God began to show me that the prosperity message when preached without righteousness as the prerequisite—without His righteousness, without Him at the center—becomes heresy! And I knew what my next assignment was going to be. God revealed to me that I was going to get up from my sick bed and carry revival across the nation. Each day, I could feel Him packing my spirit with this next mantle. Revelation 3:14–22 AMP became my breakfast, lunch, and dinner.

> *And to the angel (messenger) of the assembly (church) in Laodicea write: These are the words of the Amen, the trusty and faithful and true Witness, the Origin and Beginning and Author of God's creation:*
>
> *I know your [record of] works and what you are doing; you are neither cold nor hot. Would that you were cold or hot! So, because you are lukewarm and neither cold nor hot, I will spew you out of my mouth!*

For you say, I am rich; I have prospered and grown wealthy, and I am in need of nothing; and you do not realize and understand that you are wretched, pitiable, poor, blind, and naked.

Therefore I counsel you to purchase from Me gold refined and tested by fire, that you may be [truly] wealthy, and white clothes to clothe you and to keep the shame of your nudity from being seen, and salve to put on your eyes, that you may see.

Those whom I [dearly and tenderly] love, I tell their faults and convict and convince and reprove and chasten [I discipline and instruct them]. So be enthusiastic and in earnest and burning with zeal and repent [changing your mind and attitude].

Behold, I stand at the door and knock; if anyone hears and listens to and heeds My voice and opens the door, I will come in to him and will eat with him, and he [will eat] with Me.

He who overcomes (is victorious), I will grant him to sit beside Me on My throne, as I Myself overcame (was victorious) and sat down beside My Father on His throne.

He who is able to hear, let him listen to and heed what the [Holy] Spirit says to the assemblies (churches) (AMP).

God said to me, "For the last ten years, many have sought My hands. Now I want those that are Mine to seek My face [My character and My ways], because the end is nigh!"

I didn't share this with anyone. I kept it to myself and waited for God to release me into this mantle of revival *until one night* (while having dinner with my husband), we were saying to each other how far the Lord had brought us. My husband talked about his lean days and I shared about mine. Then I said, "You know, honey, when I lost everything that I thought was my security, God purified my motives for serving Him. I no longer sought God for things; I began to seek Him for Him! And as I continued to grow in the Lord, *things* were just *added* without my even asking! This scripture became true, '...No good thing will He withhold from those who walk uprightly'" (Ps. 84:11 AMP).

Then my husband began to share with me the revelation about *soul growth*. Afterwards, I told him, "You need to put that in a book!" It was such an *on point* word for this hour! I began to share with him what God had shown me while I was recuperating. I knew God hadn't given me the grace to write it, but instead, to preach it!

So when the opportunity came for my husband to put this revelation in a book, I asked him if he would allow me to write the foreword—not because we're married, but because I believe anyone who reads this book will be challenged concerning their motives to serve God. As you read this book, you'll be enlightened and brought to a new level of understanding concerning the necessity for *soul growth*. And you'll come to understand that if you walk according to the prophetic code of God, you *cannot* and *will not* be denied. Like me, you'll wholeheartedly embrace Revelation 3:18: "...to purchase from Me gold refined and tested by fire, that you may be [truly] wealthy..." (AMP).

INTRODUCTION:
PRINCIPLES OF THE
PROPHETIC CODE

Prosperity...what does it really mean? How does it apply to your life? How can you fully understand God's purpose and design except for studying it through the eye of Scripture? These are vital questions that you must understand *and* address to fulfill your destiny in God, and the reason I've written this book. Through the eye of Scripture we view how to prepare for and acquire biblical prosperity and wealth, which I deal with primarily in this book, and how to manage prosperity, because you cannot maximize your resources unless you manage them effectively.

The challenge lies in how you interpret what God has already revealed. So in this book, I start at the beginning to help you develop an understanding of the Bible on a level different from the levels on which it is normally viewed. To begin, the Bible is written in three major dimensions: *inspiration,* divine infusion of ideas or instructions into the human mind; *revelation,* divine disclosure of previously unknown truth; and the *prophetic,* descriptive of the communicated will of God or future events disclosed by divine inspiration through a human being (code). Each is birthed by the Holy Spirit, because on every level the Bible always reveals new seasons to come. While many great books have been written on the first two dimensions, few have been presented from a prophetic perspective. In this book, I describe to you a style of dissecting the Scriptures and receiving impartation by viewing them with a seeing eye and listening with a hearing ear to the prophetic voice in which they were written.

Through many years of teaching homiletics and hermeneutics at Bethel Bible Institute in Wilmington, Delaware, I've developed a fond appreciation of the art and science of Bible interpretation and sermon preparation. However, I've come to recognize from Proverbs 4:7 that in all of our "getting," we must learn how to "get understanding" on multiple levels…"line upon line" and "precept upon precept" (Isa. 28:13).

The prophetic code, the highest dimension of scriptural interpretation, consists of elements within the literal text that fit together to form additional meanings, revealing layers of truth for greater understanding. For example, the Old Testament passages that point prophetically toward the birth, life, death, and resurrection of the coming Messiah contain direct prophecies and prophetic types. Types and shadows are forms of the prophetic code. Certain patterns and systems of numbers are other examples. By learning the prophetic code and interpreting Scripture according to it, we begin to see the vast magnitude of the redemptive work God provided through the Messiah, Jesus, and the opportunity for application by those of us who receive Him.

Reading gives you the *milk* of Scripture. Studying reveals the *meat*. Prophetic revelation—because it is the highest level—unlocks the *deep mysteries* of God. So far, the body of Christ has tapped into the realms of *milk* and *meat* concerning this message of prosperity, but for various reasons we've avoided (or failed to embrace) the real truth on this matter. And the prophetic code can be difficult to receive because it takes time and hard labor to gain deeper insight.

With this in mind, let me explain the basis of prophetic biblical numerology (at the heart of the code of prophetic interpretation). Prophetic patterns run throughout the Bible in the form of the basic numbers. Each number has a specific meaning that becomes clearer the more you study and meditate upon the Word. For example, *one* is *whole*: nothing needs to be added to it. *Two* represents *divine agreement*. *Three* is *resurrection and completion*. *Four* is the number of *supernatural impartation*. *Five* represents *grace*. *Six* is the number of *man*, and *seven* is the number of *perfection*. *Eight* represents *new beginnings*, and *nine* represents *birthing*. *Zero*, the number of *eternity*, is without end. As you read this book, you'll see references to the biblical numbers [usually enclosed in brackets]. Before long, you'll be able to see the continuity of God's voice through recognizing the prophetic numbers.

Take, for example, an 8 x 10 puzzle. If you cut it into seven pieces, a young child could put it together because the child is able to recognize the corners, edges, and colors. If you take that same 8 x 10 puzzle and cut it into eighty pieces, a young child couldn't put it together, but a teenager could do it with some difficulty because connecting the smaller pieces takes a lot more skill and understanding. The smaller the pieces, the more time and attention it will take to solve the puzzle. And the process can't be rushed.

Let's take it further. Imagine that same 8 x 10 puzzle is cut into eight hundred pieces. It will require mastery-level skill to analyze, interpret, and reconstruct the picture. Even though there are obvious clues in the many curves, indents, corners, and straight edges, at this level you must take time to master color and positioning. Added to this, you need the vision and revelation of experience to gather and join the pieces. *Notice the picture never changes, but the skill and method needed to reveal it increase as details become more obscure.*

Although it's a careful process, as you study prosperity in light of the prophetic code, you will gain a better understanding of how the Old Testament relates to the New Testament on this topic. More importantly, you'll profit in general by becoming more aware of and knowledgeable in your spirit concerning the things of God. Some of the truths I present in this book will definitely take your mind to new depths of mystery and revelation.

My deepest burden is in firmly believing that the prosperity message hasn't been revealed to the body of Christ in its fullest detail. As we study prosperity in light of the prophetic code, its true significance will come to light. During my years of teaching biblical interpretation, I became increasingly aware of the importance of the prophetic code, this form of communication God provided to reveal additional levels of truth to us and help us fulfill our destinies in Him. To understand the nature of the true prosperity He has intended for His children to have from the beginning, He reveals to us how to prepare for, acquire, manage, and use it to help us help others.

In the early twentieth century, the prosperity message was mostly taught on the *milk* level because there was widespread poverty in the Pentecostal/charismatic community. Since there weren't many millionaires, the message was limited by the community's own experience. By late 1970 to the early part of the eighties, the message of prosperity took off because God had blessed many believers due to their increased faith in Him. However, I've found there is still a great disparity between (if I may use the terminology) the upper class, the middle class, and the poor.

The truth is, the Bible decrees that prosperity is given to all. God gives His people the power to gain wealth (Deut. 8:18), or the opportunity to prosper. The question is, who has been taught how to use this God-given power in order to maximize every opportunity? God hasn't failed in presenting to us how to do this. We have failed because, by and large, we've forgotten that prosperity is God-given.

You can't receive what you don't believe, and you can't activate what you negate. You have to act on the opportunities God gives you, or you could delay or even forfeit His promises. Furthermore, you could reap rich benefits on every level if you just hear and obey His voice.

As you study Part 1 of this book, *The Torah of the Soul*, remember that Moses received the Torah (first five books of the

Bible) directly from God during his encounter with Him on Mount Sinai. According to Hebrew thought, *The Chumash* (a collection of the five books of the Torah) tells us that the Torah is considered to be the charter of mankind's mission in the universe.[1] Messianic Jews believe the Torah is the embodiment of Christ.[2] Therefore, as you read through the first five chapters of this book—prophetically drawn from principles in Genesis, Exodus, Leviticus, Numbers, and Deuteronomy—know that Christ *in you* is the hope of glory (see Col. 1:26-27).

Part 2 focuses prophetically on accessing, acquiring, and activating God-given wealth principles in your life. It's based on truths that God revealed to Joshua when he led a new generation of Israelites into the Promised Land. These solid principles are as relevant and revelatory today as they were in Joshua's time.

In closing, I pray that you will discern the prophetic code for biblical prosperity through "opened" eyes—unveiled by the Holy Spirit. I challenge you to read every chapter prayerfully and intently. Let your mind open up, because the truths I'll be sharing with you are beyond *milk* and *meat.* Each *mystery* is carefully unlocked through the prophetic voice; each reveals powerful prophetic code principles.

Amos 3:7 says, "Surely the Lord God will do nothing, but he revealeth his secret unto his servants the prophets." So the Lord has a demand within the protocol He has chosen to reveal Himself. From ancient times until now, it takes a prophet's voice to decree that a new move of God has entered His kingdom realm *and* the hearts of His people.

Do You Need Another Copy of the SBC SMART Yellow Pages®

Our records show that you have new or changed telephone service, and that you have previously received the current SBC SMART Yellow Pages. If you need another copy, **please contact us at:**

1-866-847-2461

This is a toll-free call to our automated order system. When you call, you will be asked for your order number and PIN that are printed on the other side of this card.

DG0404

SBC SMART Yellow Pages®
One SBC Center, Rm 12-D-4
St. Louis, MO 63101

*Here's important
information about your
new telephone service!*

Order Number: (SWB)
610535285
PIN: 5332

I announce to you today as a prophet of God that by purchasing this book, you've entered the prophetic realm. As you read, I pray the message will liberate your spirit to believe that prosperity is for you, especially when balanced with the understanding that your soul must prosper *first*, then it will attract its physical counterpart to you like a magnet. "But seek ye first the kingdom of God, and his righteousness; and all these things shall be added unto you" (Matt. 6:33). *Even As Your Soul Prospers*, true prosperity will come into your life! Enjoy.

PART 1

THE TORAH OF THE SOUL—
REALIZE YOUR PURPOSE

1

THE LAW OF CREATION

Beloved, I wish above all things that thou mayest prosper and be in health, even as thy soul prospereth (3 John 2).

It's pitch black, like midnight, and the waves are churning out of control. Something's moving—no, *hovering*—all around you. Everything seems like it's about to change for the worst. You think, "No! This can't be happening to me!" Things are churning, twisting, and moving all around you, and then suddenly, everything turns upside down—*again*. Who got you into this mess? You don't know now, but when you find out—and somebody turns the lights on—you're going to give *them* a piece of your mind! You're trying everything you know to find a path that will lead you into daylight, but it's too dark, too cold. Your hands grope blindly for a place to rest, but there's nothing to hold on to. It seems there's no escape.

Now that I've got your attention, let me ask you a question. As you read through this experience, did it remind you of how you felt on any given day? If so, let me invite you on a journey into your soul. There's good news! God can transform your

1

"chaos" into a new beginning. You see, sometimes turning upside down is the only way to end up being the *right* person in the *right* place at the *right* time. Oh yes, it's a mystery. One huge, complex puzzle. But again, there's good news. God holds the key that will unlock the mystery and bring a powerful revelation.

That black, churning mass represents the dawn of creation as told in Genesis 1, but it also symbolizes a soul that's lost without God. So many people are groping for truth, building their own dreams, climbing the ladder of success, and to their dismay, they come up empty every time. Do you feel like one of these people? Then I strongly encourage you to keep reading. This part of the book will apply especially to you.

Are your finances a mess? Are you struggling with anger or depression? Have you lost close friends and family members? Do you feel a void somewhere deep within that nothing or no one has ever been able to satisfy? Are you not sure anymore what everything's all about, or why you're even in this mess? Then I urge you to keep reading.

You see, that black, churning chaos represents your life without a *vital, living, breathing* relationship with God and His Son, Jesus Christ. From the beginning He created you to be a *living soul*—full of life, joy, and abundance. But when the original man committed the original sin, man was separated from God, the Source of abundance. That's why so many people today feel incomplete; and whether they admit it or not, they're trying to find the path that leads to abundant life. In searching for a way to feel complete, people often pursue material prosperity;

when actually, they are hungering for a relationship with God and an abundant life that comes from prospering their souls.

I have great news—through Christ, you can find the real path to prosperity. And if you let Him guide you, this time it will be different. This time you'll know that presence hovering above you is the Holy Spirit, and He's ready to begin God's work *in you* at the sound of the Father's voice. Now when each of those golden opportunities come your way, you'll be ready to recognize and seize every one in order to maximize it to its full potential. Finally, you'll know who you are and where you are going—and your life will never be the same.

It doesn't really matter if you are a believer or not, because whether you are or not, Jesus is always the answer. Everybody's dealing with sin in different ways and on different levels; but if you really know God, you can learn to access Him on every dimension. And you'll finally come to grips with your past, present, and future.

If you don't have a personal relationship with Jesus Christ, I believe you picked up this book because Jesus is knocking at the door of your heart. I believe He's standing at the inner chambers of your soul. And finally, I believe He's calling you to an intimate relationship with Him, so that He can fill the void in your soul and put you back together again—the way God originally intended.

So join me on a journey into the depths of your soul and discover the path that leads to true success and abundance. The air will clear, and you'll see the light as it starts to reflect across the waters. On the way you'll learn a great deal about the Lord, the Bible, and yourself. And you'll discover that with God all things are truly possible. Yes, God has definitely equipped you to prosper.

The Genesis of Life

In the beginning, God established the genesis of the soul:

And God said, Let us make man in our image, after our likeness: and let them have dominion over the fish of the sea, and over the fowl of the air, and over the cattle, and over all the earth, and over every creeping thing that creepeth upon the earth. So God created man in his own image, in the image of God created he him; male and female created he them (Gen. 1:26–27).

And the Lord God formed man of the dust of the ground, and breathed into his nostrils the breath of life; and man became a living soul (Gen. 2:7).

In other words, the soul (Adam) became the complete snapshot of everything God is to man—present ("is"), past ("was"), and future ("will be"). Adam's soul carried the absolute ability to reference God on every dimension—the historical, the now, and the future—all at the same time. He was born into eternity and his soul was timeless. It was living. It was perfect. And it was joined with dust.

In the Hebrew, the word "dust" is described as "clay, earth, mud…." One of the root meanings is "to pulverize."[1] So why was Adam a *living* soul? Why was his soul perfect? First, he received the breath of life from God Himself. Second, it was received into a vessel that had already been broken—*pulverized.* Adam was created a perfect, broken vessel, and he had perfect communion with God. Adam was a *living* soul because the strength of God had been "made perfect" in Adam's weakness (see 2 Cor. 12:7–9).

Adam, the first soul, was made in the "image" and "likeness" of God. If I wanted to join and paraphrase the Hebrew meanings of these two words, I'd put it like this: "Adam was 'overshadowed' by the 'form' of God and was shaped to resemble Him." The word *image* is from the root meaning, "to shade," and the word *likeness* means "resemblance...model, shape...."[2] Adam was flawless.

God "puffed" (in Hebrew a root meaning of "breathed" is "to puff")[3] and Adam received the "breath" of life ("divine inspiration, intellect...soul, spirit").[4] When Adam sinned, he died to eternity. His soul and spirit were separated from God, and his body became mortal. When Adam sinned, he became a dead man walking—void of eternal life—*but God never changed.*

> *For as the heavens are higher than the earth, so are my ways higher than your ways, and my thoughts than your thoughts. For as the rain cometh down, and the snow from heaven, and returneth not thither, but watereth the earth, and maketh it bring forth and bud:...So shall my word be that goeth forth out of my mouth: it shall not return unto me void, but it shall accomplish that which I please, and it shall prosper in the thing whereto I sent it* (Isa. 55:9–11).

When God breathed into Adam's nostrils, he received perfect abilities to exercise perfect dominion in the earth. God equipped him to prosper. When Adam sinned, prosperity was lost—but not forever. First Corinthians 15:21–22 says, "For since by man came death, by man came also the resurrection of the dead. For as in Adam all die, even so in Christ shall all be made alive." God's creation would yield a return in the person of Jesus Christ.

"For God so loved the world, that he gave his only begotten Son, that whosoever believeth in him should not perish, but have everlasting life" (John 3:16). During Jesus' final moments on the cross, the disciple Luke recorded, "And it was about the sixth hour, and there was a darkness over all the earth until the ninth hour. And the sun was darkened, and the veil of the temple was rent in the midst. And when Jesus had cried with a loud voice, he said, Father, into thy hands I commend my spirit: and having said thus, he gave up the ghost" (Luke 23:44–46).

Jesus, the perfect sacrifice, put His Spirit in God's hands. And though His soul ("breath of life") left Him, it ultimately returned to God—but far from empty, definitely not "void." He went to hell, reclaimed the keys of hell and death, and restored them to the Father (see Ps. 16:10, Rev. 1:18, Matt. 27:51–53, and Col. 2:15). His body was laid in a tomb on earth (Acts 10:40). On the third day, Jesus reconstructed the pieces and completed the prophetic process when God raised Him from the dead (Matt. 27:60).

Let me put it all together. Adam created a void that only Jesus could fill. Death had separated man from God in the Garden—so Jesus brought provision for restoring man—spirit, soul, and body—back together with God through forgiveness of sin by restoring holiness (through His life on earth) and return-ing—spirit, soul, and body—to God in His resurrection. The veil that separated man from God at the entrance of the Holy of Holies in the Temple was torn from top to bottom when Jesus died, but to this day, His body still hasn't been found. Only what many believe could be a "resemblance" of Him has been discov-ered, imprinted in a white linen *shroud*—a word that means, "to veil in obscurity or mystery."[5]

In John 20, Christ reappeared to the disciples and some-thing significant took place: "Then said Jesus to them again, Peace be unto you: as my Father hath sent me, even so send I you. And when he had said this, he breathed on them, and saith unto them, Receive ye the Holy Ghost" (vs. 21–22). Not long after, they were filled with power to accomplish the mission God had originally given to Adam (Gen. 1:28 and Acts 1:8).

Jesus released the "breath of life" (the Holy Spirit), and not long after, the disciples were filled with power by the Spirit to walk in His purpose. Three thousand souls were saved, God received a mighty return on His Word, and true prosperity was born again. "Yet it pleased the Lord to bruise him; he hath put him to grief: when thou shalt make his soul an offering for sin, he shall see his seed, he shall prolong his days, and the pleasure of the Lord shall prosper in his hand" (Isa. 53:10).

Jesus is perfectly able to restore your soul. Hebrews 4:12 says, "For the word of God is quick, and powerful, and sharper than any twoedged sword, piercing even to the dividing asunder of soul and spirit, and of the joints and marrow, and is a dis-cerner of the thoughts and intents of the heart." In other words,

He knows you better than you know yourself, and because He is the Word (see John 1:1,14), He can enter your soul through the Holy Spirit—*the heart of God*—and release divine prosperity into the natural realm *from the inside* out.

Adam lost the "eternal" aspect of his soul and spirit as part of the curse in Genesis 3:19. And since God is a Spirit, Jesus came to earth, completed the prophetic process, and then sent the Holy Spirit to reconnect the "eternal" heart of God with the mortal heart of man—*to guide us back to the truth of soul domin-ion.* When you have dominion over your soul (your mind, will, and emotions) through renewing your mind to the Word (see Rom. 12:2), your soul is in agreement with your spirit, the Holy Spirit, and the Word of God. And that kind of unity brings the power and prosperity of God into your life.

Let me pause to clarify. My wife, Dr. Juanita Bynum Weeks, wrote a book entitled *Matters of the Heart.* While writing this book, she learned the natural heart has its own nervous system called the "brain of the heart." Science has also proven that the heart is formed before the brain comes into existence. It can also keep beating after the brain is dead.[6]

What's the significance? God reunited the heart (spirit) and soul (brain)—mind, will, and emotions—with Him through Jesus Christ, who, in turn, released God's Spirit back into the earth to "fill" mortal hearts and restore man's original status as a *living soul.* In other words, you can have soul dominion as you obey the heart of God within you—that comes through the "completed" work of Jesus Christ and the "perfected" ministry of the Holy Spirit. *Only* as you *abide* in the Holy Spirit (i.e., the "breath of life") and receive directly from the heart of God *into* the heart of your soul will you have been equipped to prosper, just like Adam.

Before He was crucified, Jesus prayed to the Father, "Neither I pray for these [disciples] alone, but for them also which shall believe on me through their word; that they all may be one.... I in them, and thou in me, that they may be made perfect in one; and that the world may know that thou hast sent me, and hast loved them, as thou hast loved me" (John 17:20-21,23). As we go deeper in this prophetic revelation for true, biblical prosperity, I pray that your heart and mind will be "perfected" as a *living soul,* and that you will reclaim soul dominion according to God's original plan.

The Daily Walk of Your Soul

One of the greatest things I'm blessed to share with you is that *now* you're a living snapshot of the "eternal" purpose of God. He literally *blew it* within you. So your soul doesn't need to search for God; it's already trying to seek Him because it knows the essence of your potential *in Him.* The dilemma comes when you have to go through what I call the "God test" to determine if you'll be accountable to walk in this soul dominion.

Going back to Genesis, God gave Adam total dominion over all the earth (1:26–28). As part of this, God challenged him with the vital task of naming every animal (2:19). Since there were most likely many animals in different geographic locations (due to climate and habitat), this was a great test of Adam's accountability. I believe this is one reason why the Bible records, "And they heard the voice of the Lord God walking in the garden in the cool of the day" (3:8). It relayed the principle that God was speaking with them on a consistent basis. So in order for God to transfer His dominion over the earth to man, He had to establish a regular time of communion with him.

In the beginning God had decreed and declared, *"Let there be,"* and "there was" (Gen. 1:3). Now He was using His voice to transfer dominion anointing to Adam's voice. He tested Adam: "Name the animals, because whatever I tell you that you're going to have dominion over, you have to speak to it—because it must recognize your voice. I have dominion over everything that I've declared *Let there be,* but since I'm giving you, Adam, dominion over all the earth, I'm going to walk with you and allow you to hear what I call each one. I want you to get what I say in your spirit, because whatever you speak to in creation shall obey your voice." Jesus did only what He saw the Father doing (John 5:19), and since Jesus was the second Adam, it is reasonable to assume that Adam operated the same way in naming the animals.

Jesus said, "But he that entereth in by the door is the shepherd of the sheep....and he calleth his own sheep by name,...and the sheep follow him: for they know his voice. And a stranger will they not follow..." (John 10:2–5). This ties in to Adam's challenge: Would he name the animals exactly what God had called them? Obviously so. "That's a giraffe...an elephant... a hippopotamus...penguin...eagle..." and every name created a perfect description of what God had made. God was able to use Adam's mouth to name the animals *because* his soul was perfect—it worked in the spiritual realm because of Adam's soul dominion: consciousness of God (spirit), consciousness of self (soul), and a revelational consciousness of the world (body).

In the beginning, before mankind fell and became separated from God by sin, God established the prophetic code principle that man would live by soul dominion, the unique status of being God-breathed. After the fall of man, Jesus came to earth to sacrifice Himself on the cross to restore mankind's connection with God. When we believe in and accept Jesus for what He did by taking our sin upon Himself then rising from the dead to provide the Way back to God for us, we receive the Spirit of God. The things of the Spirit of God are spiritually discerned (1 Cor. 2:14), and we are transformed by renewing our mind to the Word of God (Rom. 12:2).

We again have the opportunity to live by the soul dominion God intended for us from the beginning. If we work from our soul being properly connected to God through renewing our mind to His Word and being led by His Spirit rather than by the flesh, our spirits will speak what comes from Him, and we will walk in soul dominion. Yes, we can reference God on every level if we exercise the prophetic dominion He's given us by vocalizing what we hear Him say.

It's like God was saying to Adam, "If you're going to be the conqueror over lions, bears, and every enemy—all you need to do is activate My Word in your mouth. I'm teaching you the most powerful key of the universe: Whatever you decree by your voice when your soul is in dominion changes the atmosphere. Everything you speak will be as subject to your voice as it was to Mine. I'll walk with you, Adam, until your voice sounds like Mine. Then, as your voice begins to name every creature exactly as I'd name them, I'll know My kingdom has come to the earth and My will shall be done in the earth through you. Speak, Adam, because your prosperity begins with ruling and having dominion over all living creatures. You're a living soul. You must have dominion over every living thing."

I can hear God telling him, "Hear this, Adam: I want you to know that I'm giving you soul dominion. Your soul can speak in line with your spirit, the epicenter of My eternal presence, and you can speak to every creature and change the atmosphere they live in. You can increase the cattle or separate the flock. You can put them wherever you want on the earth because whatever you decree with your voice must come to pass. Take your soul dominion, Adam, and begin to walk in it."

Adam prospered as long as his soul lived in God; as long as he lived, moved, and had his being in His Maker (see Acts 17:28). As Adam remained vitally connected to the Lord through fellowship and obedience, he knew *who* he was and *what* he was supposed to do. When sin cut that soul dominion status—when Adam failed to vocalize what God had revealed to him—another divine decree was set in motion (Gen. 3:1–7). Genesis 2:16–17 says, "And the Lord God commanded the man, saying, Of every tree of the garden thou mayest freely eat: But of the tree of the knowledge of good and evil, thou shalt not eat of it: for in the day that thou eatest thereof thou shalt surely die."

Adam lost soul dominion the instant he moved in his own understanding. His earthly vessel was corrupted and his soul fell from life to death. Adam could no longer decree God's Word and live in prosperity. "...Because thou hast hearkened unto the voice of thy wife, and hast eaten of the tree, of which I commanded thee, saying, Thou shalt not eat of it: cursed is the ground for thy sake; in sorrow shalt thou eat of it all the days of thy life; thorns also and thistles shall it bring forth to thee;...In the sweat of thy face shalt thou eat bread, till thou return unto the ground; for out of it wast thou taken: for dust thou art, and unto dust shalt thou return" (Gen. 3:17-19).

This set the stage for man's redemption.

Even As Your Soul Prospers

From this point until Jesus' resurrection, man's relationship with God remained on a maintenance level. Blood sacrifice was their only hope—their souls remained in a cycle of death. Jesus carried the "breath of life." Everything He said and did literally changed the atmosphere of the earth. He walked in perfect soul dominion and restored the ability for man to prosper after the counsel of God. This is why John could later declare, "Beloved, I wish above all things that thou mayest prosper and be in health, even as thy soul prospereth" (3 John 2). John recognized that Jesus always gave a measurable equation to prosperity in His teachings—an expected return when you've done what the Word of God has decreed will prosper you.

John identified, even in the early church, that many had misunderstood the prosperity message. They had missed the mark because they'd lost their divine reference point with God, where the truth of prosperity begins. You see, prosperity doesn't begin because you give a large offering. It doesn't begin because you read two books on how to get out of debt. It doesn't begin by just quoting the Word, because prosperity isn't about repeating words; it's about developing your soul. Prosperity begins when you return to God and acknowledge that *He chose you* from the foundation of the world to fulfill an eternal purpose.

I am speaking by the voice of prophecy that this is the hour your finances are going to be turned around—*even as your soul prospers.* It will happen when you begin to recognize your greatest prosperity lies within; with Christ formed in you, "the hope of glory" (Col. 1:26–27). Your soul is the place of divine appointment, where your prophetic destiny is set in motion. This is the place where everything in your life begins to change; and as you are transformed back into His image (that he originally gave to Adam), your soul dominion will steadily increase.

Jesus said, "…Whosoever will come after me, let him deny himself, and take up his cross, and follow me. For whosoever will save his life shall lose it; but whosoever shall lose his life for my sake and the gospel's, the same shall save it. For what shall it profit a man, if he shall gain the whole world, and lose his own soul? Or what shall a man give in exchange for his soul?" (Mark 8:34–37). Adam gained the world and returned to dust. He lost his soul and forfeited his destiny.

On the other hand, John revealed there are no limits to the prosperity you can gain in Christ. The words *"even as"* tell us that how we apply prosperity *in our souls* will yield an exponential return in our daily lives. So whatever you allow to be deposited in your soul should bring the expectation of interest or earning—whether good or bad.

The Process of Soul Prosperity

Let's move to Psalm 1:1–3. "Blessed is the man that walketh not in the counsel of the ungodly, nor standeth in the way of sinners, nor sitteth in the seat of the scornful. But his delight is in the law of the Lord; and in His law doth he meditate day and night. And he shall be like a tree planted by the rivers of water, that bringeth forth his fruit in his season; his leaf also shall not wither; and whatsoever he doeth shall prosper." This process is based on an equally significant prophetic code principle.

A woman recently approached me at a book signing and said, "Could you answer this one question for me? I gave an offering and I believed that God was going to bless me back, and I don't understand why after I gave everything my life started falling apart. I gave for another level in God."

I looked at her and said, "That's a good sign, because everything's supposed to fall apart if you really want another level."

Let me give you two analogies. If you hire a contractor to restore your hardwood floors, you don't want him to simply cover what's already there with shellac. No! He needs to sand down all the layers—everything that's collected on top of the surface—to get back to the original wood. In other words, many times when God starts to deal with you about moving to another level, He has to sand down issues in your life so that you can see the person He originally created you to be.

This same woman was wearing a T-shirt that indicated she owned a Bentley and a Cadillac SUV. Seeing this, I added, "Do you know the significance of what you have? You have two different cars, a Bentley and an SUV Cadillac. Did you happen to know before that model year, each plant had to shut down and start over again, completely re-tooling every area from receiving to final production (where they put the final sticker on each car)?"

I continued, "So they had to change the door handles, the screws that lock into the dashboard, the air bag type, safety restraints...in other words, if they don't change everything, an old part from a previous model could be built into a new product line by mistake. This re-tooling process usually takes about two months (generally in late June through August), so dealers can start producing cars in September for the next model year."

Do you see the prophetic principle? Whenever God's in the process of doing something new in your life, He starts breaking down everything from the past. Take, for example, when God called Jeremiah to be a prophet to the nations. One of the first things He said was, "See, I have this day set thee over the nations and over the kingdoms, to root out, and to pull down, and to destroy, and to throw down, to build, and to plant" (Jer. 1:10). Rooting out, pulling down, destroying, and throwing down come before building and planting—whether you're restoring a wood floor, buying a new car, or believing God for a new level!

Now let's go back to Psalm 1 from the perspective of how it relates to the number three...which gives us deeper insight into the real significance of this scripture. According to the prophetic code, three is the number of resurrection and completeness: Jesus was raised from the dead on the third day, the Godhead is made up of Father, Son, and Holy Spirit...three thousand souls were saved on the Day of Pentecost (see Acts 2:41), and so on.

In this scripture, there are three references made to one who is blessed of God:

1. He walks not in the counsel of the ungodly.

2. Nor does he stand in the way of sinners.

3. Nor does he sit in the seat of the scornful.

This takes us back to Adam, the original creation, and also to Jesus, the "last Adam," (1 Cor. 15:45) from earlier in the chapter. According to this prophetic number, each reference correlates to a part of our being: he "walketh" (body), "standeth" (soul), and "sitteth" (spirit). Let's begin.

First: Body

When God created Adam, He formed his body first. So first of all, the "blessed" believer—one who doesn't walk "in the counsel of the ungodly"—doesn't demonstrate that he's "yoked" with ungodly habits. His body demonstrates righteousness, not ungodly imaginations. For example, if I slid into a room like a super thug with a hip-hop dip, you'd probably wonder, "Is Bishop really saved?" Yes, you would! Admit it, because whether we like it or not, the way we walk always identifies our purpose.

You can usually tell where people have been or where they're going by looking at how they walk. By observing, you can understand what's happening in their environment. You can tell whether they're confident, timid, or even what kind of mood they might be in: excited, depressed, joyful...or if they're "hating on" someone. So when your body displays ungodly attributes, you actually reflect these things to others.

You're truly blessed when your body reflects the character of God.

Second: Soul

Now let's move on to the soul. A "blessed" believer doesn't stand "in the way of sinners." In other words, your soul doesn't sin by rationalizing that everything's perfect with you but less than perfect with others. It doesn't get lifted up because you've grown so much in God, and then find fault with everybody else. Adam fell into this trap when he stood there and watched Eve fall into sin with the serpent—after all, he'd received commands directly from God; she was the one in error.

Maybe as you read this you're thinking, "Who, me? I've never had a problem with that," because you know the struggle of dealing with your own sin on a daily basis. Be careful, though. It's easy to fall into the sin of your soul.

Let me illustrate. You can easily start feeling like you've got it all together just because you're sister-so-and-so, Evangelist Blueberry, or Deacon Cucumber. Why? You can always look around and see somebody who is "lower" than you, struggling with something you've already overcome—but at the same time, you haven't dealt with the "bigger" sins in your life! So be careful. When you think you've "arrived," it becomes a sin to your soul.

Maybe God wants to use you to encourage someone, or to sing a song, or to perform some other type of ministry. *Careful...* you'll stand "in the way of sinners" when your soul gets lifted up. Your soul can get so big that God won't be able to use you. It could be as simple as helping someone that's sitting right next to you in church. If your soul is too big, you won't be able to discern if there's trouble in his life and be able to help. Plenty of believers can prophesy all night, speak in tongues, and tell you they're Bishop-so-and-so, but they fail to discern what God wants to do in someone else's life.

We have fallen into the sin of thinking too much of ourselves regardless of our level of Christian maturity. Some people actually believe they're perfect in God! No joke. We need to take account of what our souls are really trying to tell us and understand—*we've all got a lot of work to do.*

Hear me. Don't assume everything's perfect with you just because God's using you. When you start to think you're so great at something, get ready for the effects of pride to break you down in it. Remember, "A man's gift maketh room for him, and bringeth him before great men" (Prov. 18:16), but "Pride goeth before destruction, and an haughty spirit before a fall" (Prov. 16:18).

If you want to be blessed of God, don't walk "in the counsel of the ungodly" or stand "in the way of sinners." Otherwise, you'll think you're walking perfectly before God, but your body will demonstrate that your soul is living by another standard.

Third: Spirit

This brings us to the third part of the prophetic meaning, "nor sitteth in the seat of the scornful," which relates to your spirit. In other words, you need to know God for yourself so that He can help you make it through life's tests. When Adam and Eve committed the first recorded sin, one of the first things they did was to hide from God. Years later their son, Cain, fell into scorn when the Lord didn't receive his offering. And even though he could hear God's voice, Cain ignored His counsel and killed his brother Abel (see Gen. 4:3–15). Cain was definitely *sitting* in the wrong place.

Listen. Your grandmother may know God, but her faith in God can't always deliver you, even if she's known God since she was a little girl. Bitterness can take root in you even if you've been in church all of your life—even if you're a preacher's kid or a pastor! Some stuff hit my life that I couldn't even ask my father or grandfather about! I had to get before God myself. You may have good people all around you, but there are some things God has ordained that you can take only to Him.

You have to learn how to get on the floor; get your spirit on the floor with your face before God and say, "Work with me until You prove me, until You work in me to become who I really am." You have to learn how to get through wrestling with God in the night—until you understand it only takes a night for God to change your life. Remember Psalm 30:5, "...weeping may endure for a night, but joy cometh in the morning." There are some things you must learn to endure "for a night" before God; but when you come through it, joy's going to fill your heart.

Yes, joy comes when your spirit no longer sits "in the seat of the scornful," mad at sister Willie because she bought a new home...mad at brother Bill because he's about to marry Cathy.

When your spirit gets in check with God, joy automatically shows up. Watch out! You're about to enter a new day.

Second Corinthians 5:17 says, "Therefore if any man be in Christ, he is a new creature: old things are passed away; behold, all things are become new." When the Bible says "all things" it means when you *suddenly* come through that night experience, you step into a new season of your life. So even though you were struggling with something last night, when you wake up the struggle is gone because you've crossed over from the old into the new.

You know that you're in Christ when the joy of the Lord is your strength! People that have to be motivated, kicked, primed, pumped, and dragged into the house of God don't have joy because they don't know God. They're still walking in the counsel of the ungodly and standing in the way of sinners, so they have no choice but to sit and stew in the seat of the scornful.

When "all things" have become new, you're no longer swayed by other people's opinions. Why? You've walked with God, and He's worked righteousness in you. He has perfected your soul in that area. Isaiah 28:9–10 says, "Whom shall he teach knowledge? and whom shall he make to understand doctrine? them that are weaned from the milk, and drawn from the breasts. For precept must be upon precept, precept upon precept; line upon line, line upon line; here a little, and there a little."

Human opinions can't take you to another level in God. Only He can do this. The intertwining events that make up your eternal destiny will never be infused or impacted by another person's opinion. That's why you can only go so far in God when you rely on other people's experiences. You've got to lay before Him yourself…then joy will come! I don't have to wait for somebody else to tell me when God is moving. I see Him because I know Him, and I know what He's doing—whether you know it or not. That's why I have joy.

If you've ever bought a really nice car, you know that you can go to the dealer, find a car, fill out the paperwork, get approved on the spot, and still be handed a sheet of paper with an approval number (instead of the keys to your new vehicle). Many times the nicer cars aren't kept in stock because each owner wants something different—so they make them to order. How does this relate to your spirit? How does it tie into joy?

God is saying, "I want you to know that when you came through the process of being delivered from your flesh into the purity of your spirit man, *I gave you an order number.* When I put it in your hands, I told you to just wait patiently because I know where to find it."

The last time I ordered a car the salesman told me, "I'm sorry sir, it's not on the lot. We had to keep it at the docks." The docks are safer than car lots because they have twenty-four hour patrol instead of security cameras.

I said, "Okay, when are you going to bring it in?"

He answered, "It's only going to take about a day or so to put it on the truck and bring it to the dealership." I was fine with that, because I recognized that as long as I had the verbal okay and the document stating the car had been ordered, it was guaranteed to show up on schedule.

This is why the enemy tries to approach you before you get to the "application process," before you get to the prophetic process in Psalm 1:1–3, because once you come out of your "night season" as a *new creature,* you'll have a signed guarantee that something new is about to happen in your life. "Behold, I will do a new thing; now it shall spring forth; shall ye not know it? I will even make a way in the wilderness, and rivers in the desert" (Isa. 43:19).

Fourth: The New Day

This leads us to Psalm 1:2. "But his delight is in the law of the Lord; and in his law doth he meditate day and night." Let's go back to Adam. After Cain killed Abel, Eve had another son (Gen. 4:25). The next chapter continues, "And Adam lived an hundred and thirty years, and begat a son in his own likeness, after his image; and called his name Seth" (Gen. 5:3). Stay with me here—through Adam and Eve's third son, Seth, God was beginning His process to complete His original plan and resurrect man from his fallen state. God was getting ready to make "all things" new.

Six generations later, Enoch was born from Seth's lineage (see Gen. 5:3–18)—so Enoch was actually the seventh generation of Adam, which is the number of perfection. "And Enoch walked with God: and he was not; for God took him" (vs. 24). Enoch *delighted* in the Lord and he never tasted death. He lived

365 years before God *took him* to heaven…365 (vs. 23)! (Next time you look at your calendar, think of Enoch.)

God used seven generations (after Adam) to complete the prophetic process. Now, walk with me a little further. Three generations after Enoch, Noah was born. Noah was the tenth generation of Adam and the first heir to be born after Adam's death. According to Genesis 5:29, Noah's father, Lamech, "gave him this name saying, 'This one will bring us rest from our work and from the toil the of our hands, from the ground which HASHEM had cursed'" (*Chumash*). This was in line with the Hebrew tradition that had been passed down from Adam to his descendants that the curse would last only for his lifetime. That's why Noah's name means *rest*. Adam's descendants expected the condition of the *cursed ground* to improve after his death.[7] Remember, the "old" covenant gives types and shadows of the "new," and the prophetic code remains the same.

Are you convinced yet that delighting in the Lord brings a new day? Let's tie this back into Psalm 1:1. You come into *delight* when you enter God's "rest" from completing the three-step prophetic process: walking not in the counsel of the ungodly, nor standing in the way of sinners, nor sitting in the seat of the scornful.

A "new day" literally begins as your soul delights in the law of the Lord, causing you to become everything He created you to be. That's when you'll start talking about what you delight in. You'll walk around quoting scriptures as they come up in your spirit and declaring things like, "My God shall supply all my needs according to His riches in glory….'I can do all things through Christ which strengtheneth me'" (see Phil. 4:19 and vs. 13). *You'll be delighting…day and night.*

Let's look at another angle. When you've come into *delight* in God, you will have come to the understanding that being in the center of His will *strengthens* you. That's why you can "walk through the fire" and not get burned! (See Isa. 43:2). That's how you become *more than a conqueror* through Christ! (See Rom. 8:35–37). Tell me, did the last thing you went through give you more power when you came out? If it didn't, then you can know it wasn't God's will. When you've come out of a hard situation with more power, greater peace, deeper commitment, and a greater testimony and understanding of *who* God is [in you] and *what* you're supposed to do [in God]—*only God could have given you that power.* Your spirit has come to rest in the right place. You've entered a new day of *delight.*

It just keeps getting better! Psalm 1:3 says, "And he shall be like a tree planted by the rivers of water [*remember Isaiah 43:19?*], that bringeth forth his fruit in his season; his leaf also shall not wither; and whatsoever he doeth shall prosper." Get the word *whatsoever* in your spirit, because when God tells you it's your time and season, the joy of the Lord will carry you into your destiny. It will literally possess you to do all that your heart desires.

In other words, when you're in God's season no one can stop you from doing what He's called you to do. You've got too much anointing to do it! You'll sleep it, dream it, drink it, taste it, and soak it up. Your soul will overflow with noble passion and the devil won't be able to come near you—because he was never anointed to do what you're doing! Let's return to Isaiah 43. "The beast of the field shall honour me, the dragons and the owls: because I give waters in the wilderness, and rivers in the desert, to give drink to my people, my chosen. This people have I formed for myself; they shall shew forth my praise" (vs. 20–21).

If you're in a night season, don't worry; God's going to reward you in the morning! You're going to come out of the wilderness as pure gold, saying, "Though he slay me, yet will I trust in him: but I will maintain mine own ways before him. He also shall be my salvation: for an hypocrite shall not come before him" (Job 13:15–16). Lift your hands up to the Lord and thank Him for bringing you out! Thank Him for your season of prosperity.

Tell the enemy, "whatsoever." Declare it! "So what if I dropped out of school? I'm going back to get my GED because *whatsoever* I do, I'm going to get good grades. I'm going back to Community College. I'm going to increase in God." Praise the Lord and thank Him for His faithfulness. Thank Him for performing His Word in you. Thank Him for your destiny. You are "blessed" by God because you've delighted in His Word day and night.

The Process of "Overshadowing"

Remember, Adam was overshadowed by God in creation, and Jesus was overshadowed in the resurrection. This means you're not guaranteed increase *in this life* until *God overshadows you.* The word *overshadow* means, "to exceed in importance or significance…to cast a shadow over; darken."[8] I believe this symbolizes mentorship guidance—when someone who's gained invaluable wisdom, understanding, knowledge, and might helps to guide and counsel you.

In other words, God's going to overshadow you until you become the person of His original design. He's going to guide you where you need to go in order to get what you need to have. He's going to be your eyes, and you'll see clearly as you see through Him—His view. When God overshadows you, you follow after His image, because you can't see anything else. Remember, in the sense of "to shade," the Hebrew root meaning of "image," His shadow *is* His image (Gen. 1:26).

As long as it looks dark around you, you're in His shadow. Don't be swayed by superficial things. Don't try to merely satisfy yourself with happiness. *Seek for joy.* And when it's dark, press in deeper to His presence. Go deeper in His shadow, and you'll be transformed even more by His image. When everything is bright and clear, you have to look for His shadow and stay there—because God won't unveil you until He's finished "performing" His Word. Dwell in the secret place, *abide* in His shadow, "under the shadow of the Almighty" (Ps. 91:1), because God has promised, "He shall call upon me, and I will answer him: I will be with him in trouble; I will deliver him, and honour him. With long life I will satisfy him, and shew him my salvation" (Ps. 91:15–16).

It's like going to a play. The stage remains dark until everything is set in place. It's so dark that you can't even see a glimmer of light under the curtain. And you can't tell when the curtains are going to open because they're absolutely still.

Paul and Silas prayed and sang praises in a jail at midnight (see Acts 16:25). Now tell me, how much light can enter a dungeon at midnight? You see, people want to be noticed during the performance period, but God wants others to see only Him. Then at the end of the performance, He brings them out...because their prayers wrote what they experienced. They prayed, "Lord, I need You to do...I need You to help...touch... open," and God took it all down, "Okay, all right. I'm going to close this door over here...." Then there go the props. The job— a lay off; a friend leaves you alone and hurts your feelings.... Pitch darkness.

Let's reflect back to the beginning of the chapter when Jesus appeared to the disciples in John 20. "Then the same day [of His resurrection] at evening, being the first day of the week, when the doors were shut where the disciples were assembled for fear of the Jews, came Jesus and stood in the midst, and saith unto them, Peace be unto you. And when he had so said, he shewed unto them his hands and his side. Then were the disciples glad, when they saw the Lord. Then said Jesus to them again, Peace be unto you: as my Father hath sent me, even so I send you" (vs. 19–21).

Now what does this tell you? Times couldn't have been worse; the doors were shut, and the disciples were paralyzed in fear...*they were in pitch darkness.* That's why Jesus stood in their midst! God descended into that darkness and spoke, "Let there be light..." (Gen. 1:3). They found themselves inside of God's image! And as He overshadowed them, Jesus revealed the evidence of His victory—His scarred hands (work) and feet (mission). Yes, the secret place is the place of revelation, the place of your assignment. And believe me, joy will come in the morning.

Listen to me. It's time to get before God *for yourself*. You've got to ask Him for yourself, "Am I really possessing joy, or am I just jumping because somebody taught me how to jump? Am I really beholding the truth of Your Word?" Your soul is always qualified by the proof of what you've experienced in God.

Too many people in the Church have buried their assignment. That's why they skip the service and come and go when they're ready—because there's no proof of their joy. There's no evidence they've entered the joy of the Lord. And I'm not talking about a song, a shout, and a sermon. I'm talking about *delighting* in God, even when you're under His shadow...*especially* when you're there, because after it's all said and done, only those (supernatural) things which can't be shaken will remain. God said, "...Yet once more I shake not the earth only, but also heaven. And this word, Yet once more, signifieth the removing of those things that are shaken, as of things that are made, that those things which cannot be shaken may remain" (Heb. 12:26–27).

Remember the prophetic principle, whenever God's doing something new in your life, He's going to break down everything from the past: "...root out...pull down...destroy, and...throw down..." before you can *build* and *plant* (Jer. 1:10), which leads to another part of the prophetic process to abundance.

The Process of Soul Performance

Notice what happened in Matthew 25:14–30 in the parable of the talents. There were three servants; one received five talents, another two talents, and another, one. He gave each servant the opportunity to prosper according to who they would become. Interestingly, the one with five released what he had received and gained another five talents; the one with two did the same—which means that both seized the divine opportunity and realized their fullest potential, because they increased according to their own ability.

The servant with one talent buried it. I think this reflects where the church is today. We look at what we have through unprospering souls, and our lack of understanding causes us to cancel our own multiplication process. What has it profited the body of Christ to gain the whole world (get people saved) but never accomplish what we were destined to do—build the kingdom? To do this requires the wisdom and power of God. Maybe some have buried the prosperity message because we don't believe we can live in the supernatural power of God. Yes, we even speak in tongues, shout the pastor down with "amens," enjoy a sermon and a song—and then go home and do nothing, content just to be saved and ignore the mandate of God to take dominion in this earth. We've returned to a maintenance relationship with God; when instead, He wants us to *live, move,* and *have our being* in Him.

Salvation is much more than a song, a shout, and a sermon. It's receiving the supernatural lifestyle and abilities that our "image" in God affords. Salvation is using our God-given talents to increase, multiply, and receive *in abundance*.

Let's return to the parable. The servant who multiplied his five talents was told, "Well done, thou good and faithful servant: thou hast been faithful over a few things, I will make thee ruler over many things: enter thou into the joy of thy lord" (Matt. 25:21). This exposes another problem in the church today. If my soul only desires to have a heavenly experience and is content to wait until I get to heaven to really know God—to see, hear, and be blessed by Him—then why is God prophetically saying through this parable that our faithfulness yields rich rewards *in this* life? Why is He showing us it includes material blessings, multiplication in our professions, and most importantly, receiving His supernatural joy?

You see, the joy of the Lord begins when I become increased because of my networking: my social, congenial ability to present and increase my abilities so that God can trust me to be a ruler over much in the earth. This reveals yet another prophetic code principle: The joy of the Lord is a supernatural byproduct of soul dominion.

Sad to say, many in the body of Christ have been paralyzed by burying their talent(s). Their own slothfulness has divested their only means to thrive. Now notice with me again the word "few" in the above passage. Your divine opportunity isn't determined by how many talents you have but is equated to how you utilize each one to its fullest potential. So no matter where you are today, financially or otherwise, you can't lose as long as you endeavor to prosper what God has given you.

Herein lies a powerful point. The servant that buried his talent couldn't enter into the joy of the Lord because of what God was saying in the prophetic voice, "I'm going to bring you into what your soul believed about Me. You viewed Me as a *wicked* taskmaster who had no right to reap from what I had sown in your life. You saw Me as wicked because you think the message of prosperity is wicked; and because deep down, *you think money is wicked.* You saw the ability to have divine abundance as being wicked, even after you saw abundance in Me and I gave you the opportunity to *taste* and *see* that I am good. You see that I've gained prosperity through My own efforts, but you weren't willing to work as I have worked. You want to sit idly and request from Me instead of learning how to multiply what's already yours. You'd rather receive a limited measure of talents from Me on a weekly, monthly, or yearly basis, than to use what's in your hands daily to multiply your potential for increase."

God forbid. He was saying prophetically, "You wicked servant, I'm going to put you with others who will also be weeping and gnashing their teeth. There will be cutting, slaying, bickering, bitterness, anger, malice, and strife. I'm going to put you in the place where you deserve to be put. And you chose it. I didn't. You chose that place because you didn't desire to use the talent I gave you—*you buried it.* Even as you buried it, so shall you lose it." That's why the parable ends by declaring, "For unto every one that hath shall be given, and he shall have abundance: but from him that hath not shall be taken away even that which he hath" (Matt. 25:29).

When you endure God's prophetic process of becoming prosperous, His joy literally becomes your strength. Many people don't want to endure this process because it's not guaranteed unless they contribute their own commitment and sacrifice. Let me repeat: the process of prosperity offers the *opportunity* to increase—not an unconditional guarantee. Yes, Jesus loves you! His love is unconditional…but His prosperity comes only when you choose to operate in His purpose. So if you're saved, thank Him for it, but it doesn't guarantee you'll walk in soul dominion.

It's also noteworthy that when the Lord took the talent away from the wicked servant, He gave it to the one who had doubled his five talents. Let me say to you from the Holy Spirit that many in the house of the Lord have missed the mark in gaining true prosperity. Many have become embittered with God, only because they've rejected, neglected, pushed aside, and/or forgotten about their God-given talents. Instead, they're waiting on God to keep sending unconditional blessings rather than challenging themselves to rise to a new day and enter His joy. From Adam until now, your miracle increase is resting in your own hands.

God didn't send Jesus to take back the gifts, or potential of return, that He's invested in you (see Rom. 11:29). Jesus came to give you the "breath of life" and empower you with supernatural ability to utilize every talent and opportunity God has placed within you. Jesus came to help you maximize your fullest potential by reclaiming the dominion of your soul.

Now let me close with this. Ten generations after the Flood, Abram was born into Noah's lineage through his son, Shem. Watch out, because this ties in. Noah symbolized the completed prophetic process of man's redemption, and Abram demonstrated the principle of a new day. Even before the Holy Spirit was given through Jesus Christ, Abram walked in *newness of life*. "Now the Lord had said unto Abram, Get thee out of thy country, and from thy kindred, and from thy father's house, unto a land that I will shew thee" (Gen. 12:1). Abram didn't have a clue where he was going, but God took him out of the land that He had cursed to lead him into his destiny.

After Lot "was separated from him" during the journey, God declared to Abram, "For all the land which thou seest, to thee will I give it, and to thy seed for ever. And I will make thy seed as the dust of the earth: so that if a man can number the dust of the earth, then shall thy seed also be numbered. Arise, walk through the land in the length of it and in the breadth of it; for I will give it unto thee" (Gen. 13:15–17). Let's pause here. God *rooted out, pulled down, destroyed,* and *threw down* everything in Abram's past to start the *rebuilding* process. And Abram walked into his destiny led only by the Spirit of God.

There's a new land waiting for you today, and God wants you to *see it* and *enter in*. He wants you to reclaim what He's already given you. It's time to move out of the past and into your eternal destiny. And as you walk through this land, I'm going to help you examine every part of it from the perspective of the prophetic code that leads to true abundance. Now let me close with Galatians 3:1–9 (*emphasis mine*).

O foolish Galatians, who hath bewitched you, that ye should not obey the truth, before whose eyes Jesus Christ hath been evidently set forth, crucified among you? This only would I learn of you, Received ye the Spirit by the works of the law, or by the hearing of faith? Are ye so foolish? having begun in the Spirit, are ye now made perfect by the flesh? Have ye suffered so many things in vain? if it be yet in vain.

He therefore that ministereth to you the Spirit, and worketh miracles among you, doeth he it by the works of the law, or by the hearing of faith? Even as Abraham[9] believed God, and it was accounted to Him for righteousness. Know ye therefore that they which are of faith, the same are the children of Abraham. And the scripture, foreseeing that God would justify the heathen through faith, preached before the gospel unto Abraham, saying, In thee shall all nations be blessed. So then they which be of faith are blessed with faithful Abraham.

The voice of the Lord is coming to you from the cool of the garden…will you hearken unto Him and obey?

Pray, "Father, I pray that my spirit, soul, and body come in line under Your shadow in Jesus' name. Amen." Now give Him praise, because you're coming into alignment with God's original purpose. You're setting yourself up for divine increase.

2

~~~~~~~~

THE LAW OF EXPANSION

As the hart [deer] panteth after the water brooks, so panteth my soul after thee, O God. My soul thirsteth for God, for the living God (Ps. 42:1–2).

Soul understanding operates on different dimensions: it touches the reality of who (we know) we are in truth, what we desire for the future (because it understands that eternal desire is birthed in God), and also where we've been with God. The soul understands the legacy of the spirit realm that births us into the anointing we're experiencing *right now,* so it seeks to protect this anointing—and our future destiny—by gently keeping us aware that we must communicate consistently with the Lord. This is how we come into expansion.

With this in mind, we're continuing the journey on the path to abundant living by walking the "length" and "breadth" of the land, as God had spoken to Abraham. Remember the land had been cursed after Adam's sin, so the only way to walk on the land according to God's original purpose was by grace and faith in Him. That's why Abraham had to begin calling "on

~~~~~

the name of the Lord" (Gen. 13:4). Without a deep, abiding relationship with the Lord, Abraham would never have been able to walk in *newness of life* and pass a righteous lineage down to future generations.

Now say to yourself, "Rivers of living water." When you pass from death into life, God often uses a river to prophetically represent entering the eternal realm. So Abraham walked with God and brought a river of blessing to future generations: "Blessed is the man that walketh not in the counsel of the ungodly, nor standeth in the way of sinners, nor sitteth in the seat of the scornful. But his delight *is* in the law of the Lord; and in his law doth he meditate day and night. And he shall be like a tree planted by the rivers of water, that bringeth forth his fruit in his season; his leaf also shall not wither; and whatsoever he doeth shall prosper" (Ps. 1:1–3).

Receiving a New Revelation From God

Now we move to the book of Exodus where the Lord demonstrates His power in a new way by revealing Himself to Moses, a man who had to start believing, not because God had walked with him, but because he would now be required to turn and walk toward God. In doing so, Moses became the prophetic prototype for our souls to begin to "pant after" God according to Psalm 42:1, "As the hart [deer] panteth after the water brooks, so panteth my soul after thee, O God."

In this divine process, Moses was traveling to a place of pure deliverance from Pharaoh's house simply by drawing closer to God. You may remember the story. He was born into slavery and after three months was placed in a *river* to escape being killed by the Egyptians. Moses was placed in living waters. "And when she [his mother] could not longer hide him, she took for him an ark of bulrushes, and daubed it with slime and with pitch, and put the child therein; and she laid it in the flags by the river's brink" (Ex. 2:3). Moses was placed on the edge of land (earth), by water (eternity). And when his *season* came—after being adopted by Pharaoh's daughter, murdering an Egyptian soldier, fleeing for fear of his life from Egypt, and living in the desert for forty years in Midian—*God called him.* Do you see the pattern? God *overshadowed* Moses, which prepared him to be a man of destiny.

> *Now Moses kept the flock of Jethro his father in law, the priest of Midian: and he led the flock to the backside of the desert, and came to the mountain of God, even to Horeb. And the angel of the Lord appeared unto him in a flame of fire out of the midst of a bush: and he looked, and, behold, the bush burned with fire, and the bush was not consumed. And Moses said, I will now turn aside, and see this great sight, why the bush is not burnt. And when the Lord saw that he turned aside to see, God called unto him out of the midst of the bush, and said, Moses, Moses. And he said, Here am I (Ex. 3:1–4).*

It was like God was saying, "Moses, you don't understand yet, but I must draw you nearer to Me because your soul doesn't know how to find Me. I have to give you a signal of who I AM to bring you into the place of revelation because I'm calling you to deliver My people out of slavery."

During this encounter, "Moses said unto God, Behold, when I come unto the children of Israel, and shall say unto them, The

God of your fathers hath sent me unto you; and they shall say to me, What is his name? what shall I say unto them? And God said unto Moses, I AM THAT I AM: and he said, Thus shalt thou say unto the children of Israel, I AM hath sent me unto you" (Ex. 3:13–14).

Let me recap. God said, "Now Moses, I'm in the burning bush. This burning bush represents My presence. You're going to step on holy ground as you come close to Me. Take off your shoes, Moses, because I need you to come before Me with nothing between us like Adam was bare before Me. Take off your shoes, because I'm about to reintroduce man to eternity. I'm bringing you into a covenant presence like Adam had with Me; and to do this, you have to be completely open before Me. So take off your shoes, because I'm getting ready to empower the soles of your feet. I'm getting ready to let you know that wherever you walk I'll be with you, because *I'm going to be with your soul.* And I'm going to get your attention, Moses, by proving to you that I AM eternity. I AM THAT I AM."

This is how the book of Exodus brings us into expansion. You can't come into divine revelation and not reach beyond what you've always known. Divine revelation places a demand on you to change. And if it changed Moses, it can also change you. Understand something, God didn't call out to Moses until He saw that Moses had "turned aside to see" why the bush wasn't burned (Ex. 3:4). Moses turned around, started walking toward God, and *then* he was brought into revelation. Do you see the prophetic principle?

Having gone from the king's palace to herding sheep in the desert, Moses had already been broken by the circumstances of life when God called him to service. He even doubted that he could approach Pharaoh (because he couldn't speak well), but then Moses' soul began to live in God and the fires of divine revelation transformed his life.

Revelation is the light of eternity. That is why the bush was never consumed. And the Holy Spirit is the fire of God *within you* that can change your atmosphere, if you obey. Your everyday life can be flooded with a brilliant light from heaven that's so majestic, everything will change—*because of the eternal expansion in your soul.* If it happened to Moses, it can happen to you.

Through that burning bush experience, God wanted Moses to discover how eternity could show up in the earth, and then He wanted Moses to explain it to others. And the best way for him to do that was to experience it for himself—in other words, let it transform his own life. The fact is, however, that after losing great riches and starting over from nothing, Moses had lost his self-esteem. God, on the other hand, saw Moses in his greatness. He saw him as a "faithful servant," a man from a palace who'd faithfully herded sheep in the middle of nowhere for forty years. To God, Moses was ripe to reap a great return (see Matt. 25:21). And in everything he'd owned and lost, God was revealing to Moses that his soul was his most precious possession.

Letting Go of the Past

I can hear God saying, "Let me reveal a great truth to you, Moses. In the midst of every fiery dart and trial that has come against you...I've been protecting your future. Every purpose that I've ordained for you will now come forward and begin to move you toward your divine destiny." *Here's a prophetic code principle:* You'll never prosper in the fullness of God if you cling to limited experiences that are traditional in their inception, conception, and reality of experience. When God gave Moses divine insight, Moses' lack of self-esteem caused him to react abnormally. He did not believe that he was the man God thought he was. If you're going to prosper, you must believe *you already are* what God says *you'll become.*

When He said to Moses, "Listen, I want you to recognize who's sending you. I want you to know that you're representing the eternal God when you go to Pharaoh—and make sure to tell him that I AM has sent you." This is a clarion call that resides in every soul: Whenever I AM has come, there must be expansion. That's why Jesus said in John 10:10, "The thief cometh not, but for to steal, and to kill, and to destroy: I am come that they might have life, and that they might have *it* more abundantly."

Jesus was saying, "I know who I AM, I AM come. I AM a living soul in pursuit of kingdom prosperity because I AM that holy child. I AM the holy One that was prophesied by the angel to My mother, Mary. I AM that which was prophesied of old, but AM showing up now because I'm prospering *even as* My Father has decreed that I would. So I AM come that you might have a more abundant life according to God's original plan."

This is why *I AM* must be present in you from God...because you must believe you are *whatever* God decrees you to be! Say it now: "I am that which God has decreed, and I am that which God is ordaining, and I am that which is going to become..." because if you're ordained to be wealthy, you must say it before it comes to pass. Remember how God created the heaven and the earth and declare, "I *am* a great entrepreneur...*I am* prospering in my own business...*I am* wealthy...*I am* a millionaire...*I am* a networker...*I am* empowered with education," and so on. When you decree I AM, you're referencing God on another dimension and you're ready to prosper in true abundance.

A powerful mentor once told me this story. His youngest son was listening to one of their housekeepers say that her family was going to get a house they'd been praying for. He heard her say this for several years. Then one day, one of the boy's private teachers said she'd kept hearing him say in disbelief, "Uh uh, you're not gonna get the house, you're not gonna get the house...." *His words had power because he was an owner and the housekeeper hadn't yet learned how to become one, in order to see herself in the house.* Let me say to you today, once you learn to see yourself as already *being* (I AM), you'll begin to possess all that God has for you—and nothing can negate, control, or deny your access to true abundance...because you've already become what God has destined you to be. Therefore, you already have what He has promised.

Whenever you say I AM, the Father listens for His name. And wherever His name is applied, He automatically becomes a strong tower that will allow you to stand in the midst of chaos and see yourself as being successful in that area. I AM that I AM.

Moving Into the Future

Believer, you can only prosper to the measure that you *believe* you'll prosper. So let me encourage you. God just wants you to recognize that you can start decreeing *you are* what He's created you to be already. Decree it! *I AM.*

I once went through a season of financial devastation, and it made me reflect on many things, especially the past. I'd been an entrepreneur since I was nine years old and had recognized from an early age that I prospered because of the law of obedience. When I was five years old, I used to wash the van at my grandfather's church about two or three times a day, and he'd give me about a quarter (this was around 1971 or 1972). That was a lot of money for a five-year-old! Even then, I enjoyed the perspective of knowing that wealth was supposed to come to me because I always worked hard. In fact, by the time I was nine, I was so hyped and grateful for the ability to gain increase that I'd keep going downstairs, knocking on my dad's office door, and saying, "Would you please let me talk to you about becoming a businessman?" I wanted it bad. I could really see it happening.

One day I looked at our lawnmower and realized that I could open up my own lawn service. Soon I was cutting grass throughout our area. On my first day of business, I decided to cut the neighbor's grass and then made eighteen dollars cutting grass around the neighborhood. When I got back home, my father (who is a graduate of Boston University in Business Administration) had my mother call me into the kitchen. I'll never forget it.

She sat me down at the table and said, "Son, I'm going to teach you the best way to be the greatest businessman you could ever be, and that is to honor God." She looked at the eighteen dollars and said, "All right, we're going to tithe," and she took out $1.80. Then she said, "After we tithe, we're going to take out our offering, and that's about seventy-five cents. After we do that, I'm going to make sure you replace the three trash bags that you took from under the sink, so that's going to be another seventy-five cents. Then I'm going to make sure you replace the gasoline you took out of the gas can in the garage, so that's another $2.00. And I'm going to make sure you save because the lawnmower's gonna need an oil change, so let's put fifty cents aside for a can of oil so that when you have to add oil, you can do it. And those hand trimmers you use, we may have to put some money aside to eventually replace those, so we're going to put aside another fifty cents for that."

After she was done, I basically came out with about $12.00, and not including my savings in other areas, I began to see that tithing was transforming my life. It was literally taking me to another level of prosperity, because I became a covenant keeper. I expanded into covenant. So while I was celebrating the $12.00 that I had left over, the ice cream truck came and I ran outside to buy some ice cream. The next day, I went out to cut grass and (because I'd put aside God's tithes and offering) made $36.00. That was a lot of money for a nine-year-old in the mid 1970s— so I began to celebrate the law of tithing.

I wasn't filled with the gift of the Holy Ghost at that time, and I didn't get filled until I was thirteen; but I did begin to put *I AM* into action in entrepreneurship, partly because of great mentorship. My grandfather was also an entrepreneur when he first came to the United States from the British West Indies. I'm sure because of him, my father had developed a great entrepreneurial spirit—and I began to see this mantle come upon me. When the mantle came upon me, my entrepreneurial spirit was reinforced.

I pray that there will be more opportunities presented within the church by leaders and members of the church to teach, train, empower, direct, and bring clarity in this area. Much wisdom is needed in the body of Christ about business opportunities, business skills, habits, and the kinds of "tools" that are necessary for people to embrace their full potential. Some in the church need to realize they weren't built to work a generic nine to five; that their wealth will never come by pushing a time clock on a traditional job, but instead, by following God into a new and challenging day—just like Moses did.

Needless to say, I celebrated the lawn-mowing job and cutting grass became a great source of income for me. I do want to highlight, however, that even though I'd become a tither, one day I became someone that cursed God in expansion. Listen, I'm just being honest. Never try to cheat God out of anything.

Dealing With Divine Setbacks

My father became a pastor in May of 1980. My family moved, but I continued to live in South Bend, Indiana, until I got out of school. When I arrived in Wilmington, Delaware, my birthday had just passed. One day in church, somebody walked up and gave me a $3.00 offering to celebrate my birthday. I was excited. At that time, I hadn't relocated my business activities or any of the other things that I'd been doing in terms of fulfilling my potential. So I took that $3.00, went to the candy store, slapped it on the counter, and said to the clerk, "Give me 300 pieces of candy." Well, I got cavities and my parents' dental bill was horrific. You see, I didn't give God the thirty cents. I took His tithes for granted.

Let me pause here and return briefly to Moses. Before he could enter into God's presence—and the mission God had for his life—he had to remove his sandals. He had to reclaim his original status that God had ordained through Adam. He had to take off something in order to put on something else. Think about this next time you get the opportunity to tithe in church. If you give God that 10 percent, He'll turn around and give you what *you couldn't get* without Him.

To make a long story short, Moses continued to obey God and delivered the entire nation of Israel out of Pharaoh's hands (Ex. 3:16–17). A new day had come…which meant new blessings, challenges, and responsibilities. Stay with me, this is leading us to a powerful truth. In Exodus 19, God commanded Moses to sanctify the children of Israel for two days so that He could appear to them from Mount Sinai on the third day (vs. 10–11). That was when He called Moses up to meet with Him.

"And the Lord said to Moses, Go down, charge the people, lest they break through unto the Lord to gaze, and many of them perish. And let the priests also, which come near to the Lord, sanctify themselves, lest the Lord break forth upon them" (Ex. 19:21-22). In other words, God had delivered them from a cursed existence and it was time to establish some guidelines for their new, prosperous future. When Moses and Aaron went back up to God that same day, He revealed the covenant laws (see Ex. 20–23).

Then, on the fourth day, something significant happened. And Moses wrote all the words of the Lord, and rose up early in the morning, and builded an altar under the hill, and twelve pillars, according to the twelve tribes of Israel. And he sent young men of the children of Israel, which offered burnt offerings, and sacrificed peace offerings of oxen unto the Lord. And Moses took half of the blood, and put it in basons; and half of the blood he sprinkled on the altar. And he took the book of the covenant, and read in the audience of the people: and they said, All that the Lord hath said will we do, and be obedient. And Moses took the blood, and sprinkled it on the people, and said, Behold the blood of the covenant, which the Lord hath made with you concerning all these words (Ex. 24:4–8).

After this God appeared to them: "Then went up Moses, and Aaron, Nadab, and Abihu, and seventy of the elders of Israel: And they saw the God of Israel: and *there was* under his feet as it were a paved work of a sapphire stone, and as it were the body of heaven in *his* clearness" (Ex. 24:9–10). Let me recap. God told Moses to take off his shoes when he experienced His presence in the burning bush. Now, after being delivered from Egypt, receiving God's provision in the wilderness, and obeying God in sacrifices and offerings—God revealed how Israel could walk in heavenly authority on earth.

How do I know this? A sapphire stone is deep blue, which the verse says symbolizes heaven (or eternity). First of all, the stone appeared to be *paved*, which means "to make a firm, level surface...prepare the way for; make possible; lead up to."[1] Second, it was so big and clear that it could only have represented to them what heaven would be. Let's keep going. Feet represent movement, and the feet they saw belonged to God.

I can hear God saying, "Children, this is a new day. I've delivered you from bondage, given you supernatural food and water, and now I want to show you more of who I AM by teaching you how to *live, move,* and *have your being* in ME. And because you've obeyed Me thus far, I want you to know that I've gone before you on this new path—and nothing will be impossible to you as long as you abide in Me. Whatever you do from this day forward, always abide in Me, and you can walk in the ways of My heavenly kingdom on earth."

The glory of the Lord covered Mount Sinai for six days. "And the sight of the glory of the Lord was like devouring fire on the top of the mount in the eyes of the children of Israel" (Ex. 24:17). *Why did their eyes see a devouring fire?* God knew that in forty days, when Moses came down with his servant, Joshua, Israel would have already fallen into sin. "And Moses turned, and went down from the mount....And when Joshua heard the noise of the people as they shouted, he said unto Moses, There is a noise of war in the camp" (32:15,17). This was prophetic.

You see, after their powerful consecration service, God called Moses up to the top of the mountain and kept him there for forty days and nights (see Ex. 24:18). *God wasn't moving fast enough for them.* Hey, they'd had an anointed worship service and heard the Word of the Lord—why was God taking so long to do what He had to do? They didn't want to wait on the Lord, like Moses did, so they took things upon themselves and persuaded Aaron to make a golden calf. Then they celebrated their accomplishment (see Ex. 32:18–19).

Sin has a price, and it's what Joshua called "the noise of war." Three thousand souls were killed by the sword that day. Then the Lord said, "Mine Angel shall go before thee: nevertheless in the day when I visit I will visit their sin upon them. And the Lord plagued the people, because they made the calf, which Aaron made" (Ex. 32:34–35).

When you are expanded by God and then fail to weigh the consequences of disobedience, it could curse you in a significant way. I withheld thirty cents (my tithe) from God, but I didn't learn what it meant to be cursed until three months later. That summer I literally grew another two or three inches and had to wear high water pants because I didn't have any money to get new clothes. The soles of my shoes and sneakers were ripped almost all the way around, to the point that people could see my socks. I was embarrassed to go to church; my father simply didn't have the same resources as when he'd earned well over six figures a year. And since I knew he was a great businessman, I dared not ask for anything because I knew how tight things were.

I went into prayer. Burying my face deep in our brown living room couch, I began to cry out, "God, show me where I've fallen short, because I know that I have always had money in my pocket. Three months broke? My God, no, I've never been broke for three months before." Then it came. God showed me a picture of somebody giving me $3.00, and then flashed a picture of me in the candy store—slapping it down on the counter and then eating the candy. What I saw next shook me. *God showed me I was becoming someone that He hadn't ordained me to become.*

Like Adam, I'd begun to eat of a different "fruit"…something I should never have touched. God's tithe.

Just like me, the people of Israel were young in their faith when they held that first sacrifice and offering in disdain. Nevertheless, there was a price to pay. God is good, but if you stop walking His path to abundance, you can delay or abort His blessings. Yes, for three months I heard "the noise of war."

Coming Into the Promise

Let me encourage you that if you're already a faithful tither, continue to be faithful to your local church! As a believer, giving is significant.

First of all, tithing is the offering of obedience; and second, your offering is the sacrifice that leads to prosperity. Tithing is 10 percent of your income; it doesn't change. It's an equal sacrifice for the one that makes a thousand dollars a week, or a hundred dollars a week, or ten dollars a week. Therefore, my obedience cannot be dismayed or skewed because I feel that I have to make the same sacrifice as others do.

A lot of preachers say, "Come and pay God your tithes." That's not what the book of Malachi says! It tells us to, "Bring ye all the tithes into the storehouse" (Mal. 3:10). When you *bring* something to someone, you're honoring that person. When you pay someone, it means you owe something (that maybe you should have never owed). Let me deposit something into your spirit: *Bringing* your tithes celebrates who God is; it honors Him because you have to be *prepared to bring*.

I have found that people who *bring* tithes begin to operate in a manifested level of experience with the Lord. In other words, they begin to see the windows of heaven opened in every area of their lives. Listen. God can pour out such rich blessings in your life that you'll feel you can't receive any more! It will boggle your mind when He showers you on every side. And you'll become a testimony that whatever God has ordained will come to pass.

My offering tells God how much I've prospered from the last time I received an increase on my income. It represents the covenant of my prosperity. You can never prosper above the level of your offerings. For example, if you make a thousand dollars a week and give God two dollars (after you tithe), it's because you've chosen where you want to prosper. You've chosen to prosper at Saks Fifth Avenue, Neiman Marcus, Sears, Wal-Mart, or some other place—instead of prospering in God.

Let me present you with an opportunity. The next time you go to the house of God, decree in covenant with Him that as you begin to expand, as you become the person He's ordained you to be, that you'll prepare Him an offering—because that will represent what you have in abundance. And that's what God deserves. Whoever the I AM is in your soul will always be represented by the type of offering you present. If you present a small offering, you have a small understanding of I AM…if you give a generous offering, you have a deeper understanding of I AM. And like Cain and Abel, your I AM in God will be determined by the respect *He has* for *your* offering (see Gen. 4:3–7).

God presented Cain with a significant opportunity when He challenged him to do right. In layman's terms, He said, "Cain, I want to deal with you because there's something wrong right now; there's a picture that I've got to correct. If you don't understand who I AM (to know what I consider to be right), I'll give you clarity. I know whether or not you've brought Me your best and would have accepted it if you did. I AM that I AM—don't treat Me like you would just anyone else, and definitely don't do less for Me than what you would do for yourself."

Even in this correction, Cain's offering wasn't yet sin. God said, "Cain, if you don't do right according to who you know I AM, then 'sin lieth at the door'" (Gen. 4:7). It wasn't sin for Cain to bring an offering in ignorance. It would have been sin, however, for him to present the same type of offering again. *Hear this:* After God had corrected him in order to receive His favor, Cain rejected the counsel of God. My friend, please don't read this book and go back to bad habits...because for you to *know* and to not *do* is sin (James 1:22–24).

It's interesting that Cain slew Abel in the field. It was as if he decided, "I can't stand Abel living in this prosperity; I can't stand him taking his cattle out to get fat. I can't stand him growing and expanding, always overseeing and being accountable for everything he has." *And please don't miss this*—Cain was mad at Abel because (unlike Cain) Abel managed his wealth. He *managed* his abundance (we'll get to this in future chapters). Remember this principle: Whenever you give a good offering, it has to be managed. It has to be interpreted with integrity so that you can bring God your best—not what you've been able to find as leftovers.

Now we come back to the law of expansion. Your soul can only expand as much as you're willing to be taught. God can teach you how to give an acceptable offering, just like He taught Moses how to deliver a nation. The first time God spoke to Moses, He said, "Draw not nigh hither: put off thy shoes from off thy feet, for the place whereon thou standest is holy ground" (Ex. 3:5). Moses had to take something off, put something aside, to receive from the Lord and fulfill his destiny.

As you obey the voice of the Lord in your season of increase, He will lengthen your days. When Solomon became king of all Israel, the Lord came to him in a dream and promised, "And if thou wilt walk in my ways, to keep my statutes and my commandments, as thy father David did walk, then I will lengthen thy days" (1 Kings 3:14). Solomon was at the beginning of his reign, a critical time when his life had moved to a new dimension. And as Solomon obeyed the Lord, he was multiplied; but when he disobeyed and worshipped other gods, his son paid the price—ten kingdoms were taken out of his hands (1 Kings 11:29–36).

Something very similar happened to Moses. When he sinned before Israel at the water of Meribah, God would not let him lead Israel into Canaan. "And the Lord spake unto Moses and Aaron, Because ye believed me not, to sanctify me in the eyes of the children of Israel, therefore ye shall not bring this congregation into the land which I have given them" (Num. 20:12). Both Moses and Aaron died before entering Canaan (see

Num. 20:28; Deut. 34:1–5). Watch out! If you disobey God and stray from His path to abundance, you could delay or forfeit His promises. On the other hand, if you *pant after* God and obey Him, *whatsoever* you do *will prosper* through soul dominion.

Are you ready for God to expand you? Are you ready for your steps to be ordered by Him? Then pray with me, "Father, I pray that You'll expand my insight and obedience in following Your path to true abundance. Help me to bring You an offering that You'll accept and respect, because You are the great I AM, and I know that whatever I bring as an offering will be measured back to me on that level. Thank You for giving me the opportunity to grow and expand by empowering my faith in You. Help me to prosper and live in abundance even as my soul prospers. Expand my soul so that I can go deeper in You, in Jesus' name. Amen."

3

~~~~~

THE LAW OF DIVINE ORDER

To every thing there is a season, and a time to every purpose
under the heaven: A time to be born, and a time to die; a
time to plant, and a time to pluck up that which is planted
(Eccl. 3:1–2).

One of the first things you begin to learn from God as
you walk His path to abundance is that there's a time,
a season, and a purpose for everything. And if you really come
into an understanding of this, you'll develop a balanced perspective; which leads to a healthy, balanced life. *Things will*
change—especially as you walk with God—because He's going
to bring you into divine order. Let's go to Romans 8: "And we
know that all things work together for good to them that love
God, to them who are the called according to *his* purpose. For
whom he did foreknow, he also did predestinate *to be* conformed
to the image of his Son, that he might be the firstborn among
many brethren" (vs. 28–29).

If you're going to become more like Jesus, you have to be ready
to change. What are you going to look like as you transform?

~~~~~

What's the prophetic pattern? Jesus said, "I and *my* Father are one" (John 10:30), which leads us back to Genesis.

And God said, Let there be light (Gen. 1:3).

And God said, Let there be a firmament (Gen. 1:6).

And God said, Let the waters under the heaven be gathered (Gen. 1:9).

And God said, Let the earth bring forth grass (Gen. 1:11).

And God said, Let there be lights in the firmament (Gen. 1:14).

And God said, Let the waters bring forth abundantly (Gen. 1:20).

And God said, Let the earth bring forth the living creature (Gen. 1:24).

And God said, Let us make man in our image (Gen. 1:26).

God is a God of order. He always has a purpose and a plan, and His plan *always* comes to pass (see Isa. 55:10–11). Notice there were eight steps in the process of creating man...*a new day.* Seven of them set the stage for man's arrival...*perfect order.* So what should we look like? What *image* should we project? Ephesians 5:1 AMP says, "Therefore be imitators of God [copy Him *and* follow His example], as well-beloved children [imitate their father]."

We should imitate our Father. We should function "decently and in order" (1 Cor. 14:40) until we come into THE New Day. "And the seventh angel sounded; and there were great voices in heaven, saying, The kingdoms of this world are become *the kingdoms* of our Lord, and of his Christ; and he shall reign for ever and ever" (Rev. 11:15).

Here's a prophetic principle: If you want to look like your Father, and if you want to come into true abundance, you have to apply proper planning and execution. God didn't just throw His prized creation into a swirling, black hole. He took every painstaking step of preparation to make sure everything was in place. Then He created man. Get the picture?

This is how we're studying about abundant living: *decently and in order.* We have examined the Law of Creation in Genesis, the Law of Expansion in Exodus, and now we're looking more deeply into the Law of Divine Order in the book of Leviticus. Let me say this: Many times, when God is bringing things into order in our lives, it feels like everything comes to a stop. I'll explain this shortly.

The New Priestly Order

It became evident after the book of Exodus that a priestly place had to be established because the children of Israel had come out of bondage into a season of promise and prosperity.

> *And the children of Israel did according to the word of Moses; and they borrowed of the Egyptians jewels of silver, and jewels of gold, and raiment: And the Lord gave the people favour in the sight of the Egyptians, so that they lent unto them **such things as they required**. And they spoiled the Egyptians* (Ex. 12:35–36).

When God liberated Israel from bondage, He prospered them abundantly—*but the people still had a slave mentality.* At this point, they had abundance, but they weren't rich! They had to learn how to become rich, and the only way to do that was to prosper their souls. So in His next step, God taught them how to manage and multiply what He'd bestowed upon them. This set the groundwork for the giving of the tithe, which could only be done through a priestly order.

Here's another prophetic principle: Divine Order, being able to present that which is ordained of God back to God, brings you into balance. For example, when God decreed, "Let there be light," light appeared back to Him. When He decreed, "Let there be a firmament in the midst of the waters," it came into being exactly as He'd said. Heaven appeared before His eyes. When He declared, "Let the earth bring forth grass... herb...fruit tree," every type of plant life rose up to heaven—*to God.* Perfect balance.

Romans 11:36 says, "For of him, and through him, and to him, are all things: to whom be glory for ever. Amen." So whatever God gives you in *increase,* a part of it should return to Him—and the rest of it should be used in a way that glorifies Him! This is the lesson He was preparing to teach the children of Israel.

Prior to the Exodus, Israel had become so absorbed in Egyptian culture, they'd lost the respect of how to approach God; so He established a priestly order through Moses to heighten their awareness of Him. God wanted His people to know that He was living in the midst of them and understood their needs and responsibilities. Therein became the priestly, divine order.

The Blessing of Discipline

There's a mishap within the body of Christ today regarding the ministry. And in many ways, it's similar to what Israel had to overcome from living in Egypt. You see, we've embraced pomp and circumstance. We have gone through the charades of having great concerts, convocations, meetings, and conventions—but when we return to the privacy of our own homes, we lack the acceptance and discipline of divine order.

Without divine order, you simply lose your ability to hear God in crucial areas: *timing, design, desire,* and *destiny*. Divine order will cause you to bring a sacrifice before the Lord to His servants, to prepare offerings (like the Israelites did) against anything that could trespass against you with God—even if you're in the middle of a wilderness experience. So when I encounter someone who returns his or her resources unto God, I understand that a spiritual impartation has taken place.

When divine order becomes your signature, a mark that clearly identifies *who* you are and *what* you're doing, you no longer have to be *pumped* to celebrate God. And that's because divine order brings you into a new level of discipline. This is why certain things *must* stop, because God doesn't want you to continue doing things the wrong way. That's just more you'll have to clean up later. God has to put a *divine pause* in your life until you learn to do things the right way. That's why the Israelites came to a stop in the book of Leviticus—*for one year* at the base of Mount Sinai.

Discipline must come because God's Word *concerning you* must come to pass. Discipline is an essential part of change, because it not only concerns who you are, *it deals with who you are to become*. So it was necessary for Israel to stop at Sinai because they had to regroup—*set things in order*—before moving forward into their destiny...reclaiming and possessing the Promised Land.

Let me illustrate. If you were to enlist in the Army, you'd know in advance that your first stop would be Boot Camp—and believe me, it's nothing to write home about. This is because Boot Camp builds discipline in each and every soldier. You'd have to wake up at 4:00 in the morning, be out running at 5:00, go through calisthenics and develop the agilities of a workhorse for two hours; then have a small, quick meal, and afterwards go to classes to learn about what you're being strategically prepared to do.

Boot Camp is really where you get *blessed* with discipline. Many of us fail during spiritual Boot Camp, when God is simply trying to bring our lives into divine order. Then we wonder why we can't *name it and claim it!* We marvel when the enemy scoffs at us and says, "Jesus I know, and Paul I know; but who are ye?" (Acts 19:15). A demon said this to *seven sons* (of a chief priest named Sceva) when they tried to perform an exorcism in Jesus' name. The Bible calls them *vagabonds*, which comes from words meaning "to come all around, i.e., stroll, vacillate, veer:—fetch a compass, vagabond, wandering about."[1]

In other words, they chased after the wind. They joined every popular movement and jumped on every bandwagon that put on the best show. *They hadn't been with Jesus,* nor did they know His disciples. They hadn't walked with Him like the disciples did. They hadn't eaten, drank, slept, or lived the gospel—so how could they have expected to access its power? These seven men, even though their earthly father ranked high in the religious hierarchy, got stripped and beaten by that demon-possessed man (Acts 19:16).

Just as a drill sergeant opens his mouth and yells, "Wake up!" and gives the order to march; just as he tells recruits where to go and how to get there; just as he gives them the pace and speed they must travel—so would the priest in the new Levitical order. They would sound a clarion call, prophesy, announce the new, divine order and prosperity of God, and assess the giftings and abilities of God's people.

Discipline is a fundamental resource. It cannot be a haphazard, once-in-a-while experience of a believer. It's a tool to manage your lifestyle that will remain at the forefront of what you desire *to become* in God; because God can only use people that have discipline in character, personality, perspective, planning, time, resources, energy, and communication. These people will bless His kingdom above measure. For this reason, it's my sincere hope that believers will become more *entrenched* in the art of discipline.

The role of the priesthood was to bring divine correction, clarity, and conciseness into people's daily lives. And as the priests brought divine order between God and man, God began to bring divine order between man and his possessions. Matthew 6:33 says, "But seek ye first the kingdom of God, and

his righteousness; and all these things shall be added unto you."
Seek ye first...priorities. *Seek ye first*...a list of things that must
be accomplished *after the first* thing. *Seek ye first...then* second,
then third, *then* fourth, *then* fifth...shall be *added to you.*

If you can *seek first*—Number 1—the King's domain...disci-
pline...divine order; looking for the King's entry into His assets
(how He acquires and manages them). If you can get *that* in your
spirit *first,* then all these "other" things that the Gentiles seek
(money, food, drink, clothes) will be bestowed upon you by God
Himself! Understanding divine order (discipline) releases the
truth of the kingdom in your life and advances you to another
level—a higher dimension in God.

The Curse of Poverty

Now let's move to Proverbs 10:4: "He becometh poor that
dealeth *with* a slack hand: but the hand of the diligent maketh
rich." I'd like to emphasize the words *becometh poor* because
everyone's born with the potential to possess abundant life.
However, those who reject the process of *seeking first,* putting
God first and seeking divine order, *becometh poor.* So you're not
born poor, even if your standard of living may be lower than
middle class or less than rich. *Potential still resides within you to
become rich.* You already have *within you* the power to gain wealth.

Here's a prophetic principle: Potential and opportunities will
always present themselves, but your level of discipline will
equate what *becometh* true about the *real you.*

Remember, the *real you* is already in your soul. Nothing can be hidden from your soul. Your soul *knows* you; it's the most priceless thing you possess! However, you can become poor by dealing with a slack hand and undisciplined thinking. You can lose untold riches by having an undisciplined lifestyle and attitude. "Oh, whatever, whenever I get to it, next time, some other day, next year, *tomorrow*..." Whenever you start letting this come into your thought life, you've already minimized the level of abundance God can bring into your life.

Your soul is like a sponge. It picks up everything that flows by it. Some of these things are good, a few are great, and much of it isn't good at all. So you must recognize that your soul receives all this data—information from the world and stimuli from your senses—but it knows the truth *of you*. It knows who you've become *in God* before the foundations of the world.

Your prosperity will only be released as you seek the kingdom, the portion of your existence that's already connected in heavenly places. So your soul becomes a beacon in the earth that makes it a point of reference in the spirit realm. My wife calls this process "a divine match," because when you display a spiritual principle on earth, it magnetizes and manifests something identical from the spiritual dimension *in you*.

Every now and then you see a good, modern war movie where ground troops are used to penetrate enemy territory and set up beacons—so that when they release a bomb toward a target—it hits the bulls-eye every time; *because it's laser-connected to a homing device.* The beacon has a critical role: To literally call the bomb out of the air to hit a specific location. Here's how it plays out. A ground soldier is stationed at a distance, aiming towards the target with a radar gun. This gun places a beacon signal on the target, and a bomb is released from the air. The bomb has no choice but to hit the mark.

The same principle applies with seeking. Seeking is the beacon of your soul. And each day your soul calls to heaven for *whatsoever* God is releasing: "Thy kingdom come. Thy will be done in earth" (Matt. 6:10)...in me, in *my soul.* This is where God wants to land the explosive, *dunamis* power of the Holy Spirit,[2] to cause things to come into your favor and magnetize you towards greatness—but He only does this for the disciplined. Remember the parable of the talents? The servants with five and two doubled their portions, and the one who hid just one *lost it.* God sends power to the servants that are disciplined enough to go out and not waste time.

I think part of the reason the servant with the one was embarrassed is that he probably had a lot of time. "Well, I'll do what I normally do, because it doesn't hurt me. I'll bury this; and if I want to, I'll get to it. If I want to, I'll pick it up again, and maybe I'll get challenged enough to do something with it next year, or in the next two to three years." But the master came back; and when He did, He gave rewards to the good *and* faithful (which means that they underwent a process of consistently managing their lifestyles). Many of us want to do good, but we're not faithful. We can always be consistent to a certain degree, but being *faithful* means to be consistent even when you don't feel like it. *Faithful* understands the long-term benefits of *doing.*

This is significant, because when you're faithful in what God has ordained you to do (when you practice divine order), you become consistent in that area *regardless of how you feel*. You're faithful to exercise even when you're tired because you've made a commitment to go to the gym. You know the reward isn't just getting to the gym; it's completing the task and reaping the reward…the great feeling you get after the workout. You have to *press through* your *lifestyle* to get there, and when you reap the bonuses—better fitting clothes, more energy and strength for the day's activities, and better rest at night—it only *adds to* your well-deserved sense of accomplishment. This is what happens when you put *first things first.*

When you consider Proverbs 10:4, you have to recognize something about disciplined people: They understand that how they treat God (and the things that pertain to Him) ultimately identifies how He's going to treat them. In other words, you can't have dysfunction in your life and expect God to give you real prosperity—no matter how much you *claim it, quote it,* or *say it.*

Truth is, if I can't keep my own car trunk clean, how can God trust me to transport an important package from one place to another? I don't have room to carry it! And chances are, it can't be put in the back seat either; because that's loaded with stuff, too!

In one Sunday service, I talked about closets. This may sound funny, but closets actually identify how disciplined you are. They tell approximately how much time you focus and direct attention to your future. If your closets are dysfunctional, then obviously, you're going to be dysfunctional. *This is how it happens*—one morning as you're getting dressed (you think you have it all together), you've put almost everything on, but still need that blouse or shirt...and you can't find it. So you go through every closet (maybe it didn't come back from the cleaners)...then you search every hamper to see if maybe you left it in there—so that you can iron it quickly. And what generally happens? You can't find it. Ten minutes are gone; ten minutes have been lost.

Oh, you know how it is when you have to find that perfect pair of brown shoes that goes perfectly with *that* outfit; but you don't know if you left them at the shoe shine place or downstairs underneath all the clothes. You don't know if they're in the trunk of the car...so on and so forth...so you waste another ten minutes looking for them. On the other hand, people who know how to discipline their attire *clean, reorganize,* and always have what they need available.

How you manage your closet space generally reflects in other areas—because it's one of the most involved areas of your life! You wear clothes every day. You may not eat breakfast every day or prepare a lunch every day; you may not be home for dinner every evening—but day in and day out, you have to put on clothes. And if your closet's dysfunctional, you need to take a look at your life—it's probably the same way. If you have difficulty identifying problems and putting them together, maybe it's because your closet's telling you something. *It's hard for you to find things when you need them.*

This is a basic analogy, yet extremely practical and insightful as it concerns your spiritual maturity; because when you can't find what you need, you tend to go without. Like finding the right coat. If you can't find it, you'll jump out wearing whatever you have on...and it's cool outside. You almost catch a death of cold just because you didn't put your coat in the right closet. "Let's see, I didn't pull it out of the bag that was in the car, and I didn't put it *there*..." Now you're really confused! Did you leave it at Sister Blueberry's house, or maybe at Sister Williams' house? Face it! You have a propensity for leaving stuff in all kinds of places because you don't have the next thing we're going to talk about, and that's *accountability*.

Here's another thought from Proverbs 10:4: *Lack isn't supposed to be prevalent in the house of God!* We lack because, in most cases, our leaders lack the ability to display proper divine order. Leaders lack the ability to be on time, leaders lack the ability to manage finances, leaders fail to manage goals and desires. What's the bottom line? Leaders lack accountability.

Why is it that *everything else* in the church is so superspiritual except for the practical aspects of divine order? "I'm going to show up at church on time...bring my tithes and offerings; I'm going to worship God on a daily basis through prayer and celebration of reading His Word." Why don't we just take the opportunity to organize our lives so we'll know where to find our credit cards? Know how much money we have? Why don't we take time to clean our cars and stop just throwing things into them? Why do we have to go through the motions of standing outside without a coat on (for eight to ten minutes), trying to find it in the car—and then catch a death of cold? It's simple. We are undisciplined.

If we can get divine order back into our souls, then we'll automatically achieve a greater level in God, because now we've stepped into *accountability*. "But the hand of the diligent maketh rich" (Prov. 10:4).

As poverty is a spirit that lives through a lifestyle (demonstrated by outward manifestations), so is the lifestyle of a person that *becometh rich*, who has obtained it because they've applied discipline. This person has learned to become rich *within*.

How to Become Rich

This story always amazes me when I think of it. God spoke something to me four years ago that never left me, mostly because of the laws of wealth and where my soul was prospering at the time. For many days I'd been dealing with a situation where I acquired a 54,000 square foot complex to start our ministry. The grounds were overgrown, weeds and broken glass were everywhere, and one particular location had been neglected for several months. Having started with no members, no money, and just a big vision, I began to sweep and clean up the broken glass, cut the weeds, and so on. I found pennies all over the ground: rusted, dirty, almost unrecognizable pennies.

What was interesting is that I never found nickels or dimes—or anything else in reference to money—just pennies. Yet when I'd done the demographics and statistics in 1998 (from the 1990 Census), I discovered the ward our school/church building was settled in had a mean income of $55,000 per household, which was third or fourth on the revenue list for our area; so it wasn't bad at all.

As I began to pick up pennies, I neatly stacked them in the windowsill in my office, until they became a group of fifty. Then I rolled them together and deposited them in the bank. So I had a little incentive to keep on cleaning, and cleaning, and cleaning. Of course, it was a huge complex on a lot of acreage (with pennies all over it) that ultimately accounted to around four dollars. So I'd collected about four hundred pennies.

Then something major happened in May of that year. I attended an annual conference called *Praise Power Celebration*. At the end of the conference, I was walking through one of the VIP rooms and saw a shiny penny on the ground. (Now I was dressed in a nice, navy blue, double-breasted suit; Brooks Brothers conservative tie; a French cuff shirt, and blue gator shoes.) I was dressed to the T, and when I saw that shiny penny, I bent down to pick it up. Then God said, "Don't pick up the penny." *Of course,* I knew the voice of God and thought it strange. "Why is God telling me not to pick up this penny?" I wondered. "I've been picking up pennies for almost seven months. Why am I now not supposed to pick up any pennies?"

It was shiny, brand new, and bright...I could see it ten feet away. "I've got an eye for pennies now," I mused. It was protruded about three quarters of the way underneath the corner of a box—so one quarter of it was still under the corner tab. And I picked it up...in *disobedience* to God. I twirled the penny in my fingers as I walked down the hallway and around the corner to a production truck (that was videotaping the conference). Just then, the penny slipped out of my hand and rolled under the truck.

Still dressed to a T, I knelt down *again* on one of my knees (on asphalt) to reach for this penny underneath the truck. God spoke to me again and said, "If you pick up this penny *this* time, you'll pick up the spirit of poverty." I stared at that penny, and we had the longest, ten-second debate I can remember. Then I stood up, let that penny lay there underneath the truck, *and asked God what He was doing.*

He said, "For a season, in the midst of cleaning the grounds—because you couldn't afford a janitor or anybody else, you were your own employee. You had to pick up pennies because they were there, and you became attracted to a spirit that you were never supposed to be part of. It wasn't part of your *divine order,* and I don't want you to form roots in that spirit. And I don't want it to get roots in you." And then He said, "Pennies carry the spirit of poverty."

God started bringing to my remembrance that when I'd ever gone into a poor neighborhood, into a project or ghetto section of any city, I found that even poor people didn't hold on to pennies. Pennies lay around playgrounds, on laundromat floors, outside liquor stores and supermarkets—they can be found in any and every place. Pennies just lay on the ground. Even the poor don't necessarily pick up pennies. They have no value, so people leave them where they see them.

Pennies seem to say, "Spirit of poverty, lack, and no discipline." You see, money isn't supposed to lie on the ground; not even pennies. When people drop them, it's because they disregard accountability and the ability to manage money properly, even if it's only a penny.

Two intriguing things happened. Within twenty minutes, I returned to the VIP Room to quickly take care of something, and then stepped out of a door (that I normally didn't step out of) to find a person waiting in the hallway. This person said, "About forty-five minutes ago, God spoke to me in the midst of the conference here at the Baltimore Convention Center, and told me to write this check and give it to you...and here it is." Being real churchy (as most of us church people do), I didn't look at it, but slipped it right in my pocket. I responded, "Thank you." Don't get me wrong. I appreciated the fact that somebody would think about me, and that God happened to be speaking to that person at the same time I was gazing at this "shiny penny." While I was debating with God, He was speaking to somebody else about blessing my life!

I walked into the bathroom, opened the envelope...and it was a check for one thousand dollars! Obedience is always better than sacrifice. Later that Sunday evening, after the close of the conference, I went across the harbor to The Cheesecake Factory with a good friend. While we were waiting for a table, I happened to look down. I didn't see pennies; I saw nickels, dimes, and quarters...about $2.70 worth, and I quickly picked all of them up. I didn't let the opportunity go by. But at the same time, I noticed something—I didn't have the same spirit as when I'd picked up pennies. Why? Perceived value. Somebody's change fell and nobody noticed, versus the fact that the change had just been thrown to the ground because nobody cared. After all, they'd probably thought, "Pennies aren't important."

That day changed my life about true soul growth, especially since I'd been teaching and living according to the principles of tithes and offerings; believing that God would prosper my life and allow me to live in a level of prosperity. No, I didn't have everything, but I didn't *have to* have everything...because real abundant living doesn't start with being rich. Rich is determined by *having what I need* in life *right now.*

When God told Moses everything that would be required to build the first Tabernacle and establish the priestly order (Ex. 25–31), the challenge must have seemed to be insurmountable. Yet God had already blessed Israel with the spoils of Egypt; so He was simply calling for them to manage these possessions in order to bring an offering (Ex. 25:1–9). God said, "And let them make me a sanctuary....According to all that I shew thee" (vs. 8–9). In other words, God was saying, "I've blessed you with many possessions; now it's time to *become rich* and discover true prosperity—because as you build My house, you'll be confirming your commitment to Me."

Adam didn't have to build anything in Eden. God did all the building and then placed them in the Garden to manage it (Gen. 1:28). Then sin robbed them of their inheritance. So now we see God requiring man to assume more responsibility. God gave them raw materials, and they were to build according to His instructions. This way, responsibility would introduce them to ownership—which would ultimately release them from the bondage of a slave mentality. So if I have it, I'm rich. If I manage it, I'm rich in my soul. If I'm eighty years old and have nine million dollars in the bank, then call me rich. But if my debt is equal to my cash value, I'm not.

Let's look at two examples. On one hand there's a fifty-year-old person who's worked a number of years. He has a $300,000 house that he still owes $200,000 on, three vehicles (and he owes on every one of them), and their total in savings and investments is $10,000—and they only make $100,000 a year—their living expenses come out to about $95,000 a year. This means they only have a savings potential, or a positive cash flow, of $5,000. On the other hand, there's a single woman that makes $35,000 a year, but her expenses are only $20,000— which means her positive cash flow is $15,000 a year. Even though she earns less, she's actually *richer* than the man with a higher income. So the person who makes more has only $5,000 left over, but according to his salary, what he drives, and where he lives, he looks rich. The reality is, rich is determined by the amount of abundance you've acquired, or have the potential to acquire, and the fact that you're utilizing that potential by working it through.

When you study Proverbs 10:4, you recognize that *rich* isn't based on the *type* of things you own. Your *richness* is based on the liquidity (asset development) that you have at any age. Please, don't let age or amount of income—or what you perceive somebody else is earning—make you feel less rich. A person that makes $50,000 a year and has $10,000 in savings is richer than a person that makes $250,000 a year and has $2,000 in savings and can't pay his bills. Rich deals with lifestyle management more than how many things you have. Poor deals with the lack of lifestyle management. And then there's the next level: *obtaining wealth.*

The abundant soul will acquire much, and a soul that's lacking will experience poverty. Remember the talents: "For unto every one that hath shall be given…but from him that hath not shall be taken away even that which he hath" (Matt. 25:29). Let's take it a little bit further. *He that hath a soul of abundant living, or a living soul, shall have those things in life. He that hath not a living soul, or a life of abundance, shall lack those things in life.*

4

～～～

THE LAW OF
ACCOUNTABILITY

*Awake thou that sleepest, and arise from the dead, and Christ
shall give thee light. See then that ye walk circumspectly, not
as fools, but as wise, Redeeming the time, because the days are
evil (Eph. 5:14–16).*

A s you continue down the path to soul prosperity, it
won't be long before you come to the place of *accountability*—because your soul must be accountable to God. It came
from Him, so it must present itself back to Him. The question is:
Do you know exactly what's in your soul? Have you successfully
identified the resources He's given you to maximize your potential? If not, how can you present it back to God, or even be able
to recognize how your soul has been increased?

Just as Psalm 1 lists the steps of accountability to become
"blessed" in God—*walking not* in the counsel of the ungodly,
standing not in the way of sinners, nor *sitting* in the seat of the
scornful—you must learn to *become accountable* for your own
soul prosperity. When the book of Numbers begins, we find God

～～～

speaking to Moses two years after Israel was delivered from Egypt (see Num. 1:1). *Two* is the number of agreement—so becoming accountable to God puts you into agreement with Him...*and that's powerful*. Let me explain why.

Israel completed construction of the Tabernacle in Exodus, established the priesthood in Leviticus, and then God had a place of rest among His people. There was the Outer Court (where everyone could enter), the Holy Place (where only priests could enter), and the Most Holy Place (where the ark of God rested behind the veil). At each level there came a new level of accountability.

The prophet Isaiah declared, "I saw the Lord sitting upon a throne, high and lifted up, and the skirts of His train filled the [most holy part of the] temple" (Isa. 6:1 AMP). When Jesus came, all who touched "the hem of his garment [in other words, got close enough to touch Him]...were made *perfectly* whole" (Matt. 14:36, *insert and emphasis mine*). That means that when you've learned accountability, you'll reach your deepest intimacy with God. And His *eternal* heart will become one with every part of your soul...bringing you into a *perfected* state of soul dominion.

Identifying the Process of Accountability

So the process of accountability began. "And they assembled all the congregation together on the first *day* of the second month, and they declared their pedigrees after their families, by the house of their fathers, according to the number of the names, from twenty years old and upward, by their polls" (Num. 1:18). This reveals God's order of succession.

First, He gives you a *living soul,* or soul dominion, through receiving Jesus Christ and the indwelling presence of the Holy Spirit. Then He leads you into the expansion of possessing the power of His name, *I AM.* So you come into the responsibility of a deeper relationship with God by submitting to the Holy Spirit, which gives you supernatural power to decree the things of God in the face of your enemies. Then the kingdom of God can be released in the earth through the Holy Spirit *in you.*

The Importance of Numbers

Going back to Numbers 1:5, something significant was spoken to Moses, "And these *are* the names of the men that shall stand with you." Now let's go back to Exodus 25:2. "Speak unto the children of Israel, that they bring me an offering: of every man that giveth it willingly with his heart ye shall take my offering." Could there have been a divine connection between those who gave willingly and those who would stand with Moses?

I think so. The men who had proved themselves to be faithful to diligently build God's house were then chosen to represent their tribe to all of Israel. Remember the prophetic principle, "For unto every one that hath shall be given, and he shall have abundance" (Matt. 25:29). These *good and faithful* men continued to give. "And it came to pass...; That the princes of Israel, heads of the house of their fathers, who *were* the princes of the tribes, and were over them that were numbered:...brought their offering before the Lord" (Num. 7:1–3).

The Law of Accountability deals with integrity. And there's no way that God can test how great you can become unless He can trust you with numbers, statistics…any information that empowers you to see a "pattern" of who He is. This is why God begins to deal with specific areas of your integrity, because the closer you get to Him, the more dark areas will be exposed. "For nothing is secret, that shall not be made manifest; neither *any thing* hid, that shall not be known and come abroad" (Luke 8:17).

God simply won't allow your soul to remain in unfruitful places, where you have no understanding of divine patterns. Therefore, as you enter into an understanding of numbers, you'll discover that divine order always brings you into a level of increase. And the only way you'll be able to see the increase is *to take note of it.* Slow down, take time to digest the Word of God, lay yourself before Him in prayer and intercession—and then live responsibly outside of your prayer closet. Then your inner life will create a match with your outer expression.

Let me say it again. Soul prosperity brings you into abundant living—but *true abundance* is stabilized when you understand kingdom management. God's process through the *Torah of the Soul* helps us to understand…the creative law of dominion is in our mouths, and to *whatsoever* we speak, we'll claim it according to our voice of dominion.

This is how I've come to understand the law of anointing that flows from within me. In other words, I've allowed every part of my life to be numbered. Therefore, everything that's related to me, everything that's in relationship with me, everything that's equated with me *gets blessed,* because the anointing flows from the head of Aaron's beard down to the rest of the body (Ps. 133). I'm in covenant connection; I'm in divine placement. So I'm in a strategic alliance with the anointing that *whatsoever* I do shall prosper.

Now let's return to the book of Numbers. The Law of Accountability also brings me into the law of trustworthiness. If I can't be trusted, then I can't possess the full level of integrity in order to embrace the full abundance of God. Abundance is strategic. Abundance comes when everything has been set into its proper place.

Let me remind you: *rich* is a spirit, not necessarily an amount. If I'm rich in spirit, though I technically may have less than somebody else (in terms of net potential, because of what I earn)—*I have more net worth* if I manage my salary. There's a difference between net *potential* and net *worth*.

When you come into the Law of Abundance, you must understand that you're accountable for everything that happens *in* you, *through* you, *for* you, and *by* you. More importantly, you must know there are certain statistical, accountable aspects through "numbers" by which God will show you patterns. If you've ever dealt with numbers, you understand—first of all— the law of single eternalness. In other words, nothing needs to be added to *one* to make it whole within itself. One is already one.

Let's briefly review. *Two* is the number of agreement. When two touch and agree, divine power is released (see Matt. 18:19). *Three* is the number of resurrection, completeness, and wholeness. "For in him [Christ] dwelleth all the fulness of the Godhead bodily" (Col. 2:9, *insert mine*). *Four* is the number of supernatural impartation. *Five,* the number of grace. *Six* is the number of man. *Seven* is the number of perfection. *Eight* is the number of new beginnings. *Nine* is the number of birthing. And *zero* is the number of eternity—it's without end. Learn to develop an ability to know every number God has established in Scripture because it will lead you into true accountability.

Effective Money Management

Now let's go a little further. Another way you become accountable is to handle your finances wisely. If God is going to trust you, He wants to know that you're managing your money right. For example, if I asked you how much money you had in your wallet when you woke up this morning, would you be able to tell me? Is your money scrambled between business cards, receipts, candy wrappers, and other things in a pants pocket?

Do you organize the money in your wallet from small to large bills? Do you maintain an accurate daily accountability of how much money is in your checking, savings, or money market accounts? How about CD's, T-bills, and so on? Maybe you're penny-pinching—robbing Peter to pay Paul. Ultimately, you'll have the dilemma of not knowing how to generate more finances because you have less commitment over the integrity of what you have now.

God wants to make sure that, even though you may spend it, you know *where* your money goes and *why*. The Law of Accountability justifies this: "The reason why I did *this* is because *that* needed to be taken care of." It references through the book of Numbers that I should know where my increases occur. I know that my wealth has come because I've worked overtime, or started my own home business, or acquired a partnership. Perhaps I've decided to invest a little differently in the stock market, in private companies, or in a private venture. It's critical that you know how to deal with accountability, because until you do, God won't let you enter *your* Promised Land.

Prosperity doesn't come by haphazard confession. Prosperity comes through the process of the *Torah of the Soul.* Some things in your life have to be torn out, and other weak areas have to be removed. God has to destroy some things that you picked up from your family...a father who was never disciplined to be on time, or a mother who was never neat. Maybe you picked up poor social habits and were never very personable. *Then* areas of networking (building relationships) would need to be developed in you—because you have to be accountable for every opportunity (see Jer. 1:10).

In the book of Numbers God is saying, "I can't take you to your next level until you've become accountable, because your integrity on this level will be determined by your ability to know *exactly* how good I've been to you. You've got to know about the numbers I've given you by counting the deposits that I've divinely made in your life. You've got to order the importance of things that I've placed in your daily experiences." *Can you account for them?* Can you count the actual cost of launching that new bicycle business? Can you gain perspective of what you're going to be able to generate from that computer when you buy it—or is it just going to be another idle machine in your house that has no value after two weeks? The Law of Accountability.

Let me revisit a question: Have you looked for something that you just couldn't find? Let's say you've been looking for tools. You bought a set last year, but now you can't find any of them. What happened? Did you leave the kit outside after you fixed the mirror? Did you forget where the ladder was until it rusted because you forgot to put it back? The Law of Accountability.

The prophetic principle of Numbers has been identified: When the children of Israel were about to enter to another level and glory in God, it was because they knew how to give God His "numbers."

Some things may seem small but are extremely important. For example, how many times do you go shopping in a week, how much money do you spend on gas, how much extra time do you have? *Certain things must be accounted for.* How many hours are you wasting because of poor time management—per day, week, month? Where's the accountability for the success that should be coming into your life? You cannot achieve true success and abundance unless you have true accountability.

The Snares of a Sinful Soul

When your soul is unaccountable, it can easily fall into sin—and then to make matters worse, you camouflage it. Take gambling, for example. Is that being accountable for numbers? If someone says, "Oh, I wasn't really gambling; I was just trying to win some money" and gave their whole paycheck to win $134,000,000—that's gambling! First of all, hitting the lottery isn't your source. If you're a believer, God is your Source. Now, if you were to buy something at a rummage sale for five dollars and, in turn, got a raffle ticket; then you waited around for a drawing, that's not gambling. That's investing in an opportunity.

On the other hand, if this same five dollars were your tithes or bill money—not extra, increase, or overflow (something that could be invested)—that's when it would become sin. If you had five dollars to blow at McDonald's, then you could decide, instead, to invest it in a good opportunity.

Some people are just itching to gamble. Stay with me, because I'm telling the truth here! There are people sitting in church just waiting to hear the right numbers. "Turn in your Bibles to Psalm 1...now let's go to Psalm 34." And if the minister doesn't say six numbers, they'll go ask for the rest. "Uh, Pastor, could you quote another scripture for me?" "Sure! Isaiah 54:17 says, 'No weapon formed against you will prosper.'" *That's how some people start calling the numbers!*

The point is, when your soul is unaccountable, your actions can become uncontrollable—because they're dictated by the ungodly passions in your soul. And this is why you're not always at the spiritual level where you can embrace God-given opportunities. *Your soul has to rise to a new level before you can embrace them.*

As I am writing this, the Holy Spirit is urging me to stay on this subject, because some people have gambling addictions. If you spend five dollars a day on lottery tickets, you have a habit—a process of doing something over and over again without reason or thought of the consequences.

Think about a person with a bad habit of never stopping at stop signs. You know what happens. He nearly stops, but never lets the car stop completely, so it edges forward until it rolls through, and then he steps on the accelerator again. Do you know any people like this? They don't stop at stop signs but have the nerve to honk at anybody else who creeps through an intersection. That's how a lot of fender benders happen. Somebody just rolled through.

Bad habits shape circumstances with negative consequences. Let another car hit yours, tear it up, and put you in the hospital for a couple of days...you'll make sure you stop at the next stop sign! You'll look at that stop sign, hit that brake, and say, "Whoa." Your new reality references will make you sit there for ten minutes, waiting, looking right and left, right and left....

So if you've got a gambling addiction, that bad habit will have you sitting there every day thinking, "Just five dollars...just five more dollars," while you keep missing the numbers. That's frustrating. Five dollars a day adds up to $150 in a month's time. That's $1,800 a year—and *that* really hurts! If someone were to hand you a check for $1,800, how would you invest it? Would you take the money and say, "Give me six numbers for $1,800"?

The most serious issue with gambling is that Jesus is no longer your Source. When you gamble compulsively, you've made the "opportunity" more "god" than God Himself. You don't trust God enough to pay your tithes, but you'll throw your money away on chance.

Let's get down to it. Maybe your soul is unaccountable in other ways—you don't play the lottery, but you "play" a lot of other things. Maybe you gamble with relationships. When you see a man you're attracted to, you think, "Let me just go over there and see what he says today." You want to test that brother out, make something happen, but you won't admit it. So you glide over, bump into him, and say, "Oh, I was just coming to pick this up...*how are you doing?* Did I hear you say you were going to lunch? Don't let *me* interrupt you." This is gambling. You know what's really going on in your emotions, but you're gambling because your soul has lost accountability. You can't trust God in romantic relationships.

We can also gamble with time. Let's say you pay $80 a month for cable. You've got Cinemax, Showtime, HBO...all the channels. You never miss *The Sopranos*. You tape every episode. You've even got the Italian Soprano Channel just in case you want to learn Italian. Then you go to Blockbuster and rent movies! That's a minimum of $80 a month to gamble your time and waste precious hours of your life. Are you counting the numbers?

Let me help you. Eighty dollars a month divided by thirty days is approximately $2.50 a day. So you're paying for a $2.50-a-day habit to spend four to six hours in front of the television. How much is your time worth? Let's break it down further by dividing $2.50 by four. That means your time during each of these four hours is worth about sixty cents. Let me put it another way. *I could buy an hour of your life for sixty cents*...and that's if you pay $80 a month for cable! What if you only pay $40 a month?

I could buy an hour of your life for a little more than thirty cents. *Isn't that hour worth more than thirty cents to you?*

If this describes you, then your life has slowly become controlled by an addiction to television. Let's say this is hitting home with you right now. Start now and stop the cycle. At the end of the week, ask yourself, "What did I get for every hour that I paid somebody to rob my time?" Let's calculate another angle. Take five days a week that you spend four hours watching television—*twenty hours of your life are gone.* Twenty hours multiplied by sixty cents is about twelve dollars. You didn't even get paid one hour's worth of work on a decent job for twenty hours of your life!

Twenty hours of your life are gone, and your body's sitting there *wishing* you had a seven-bedroom house, *wishing* you were driving a Jaguar, *wishing* you were on vacation in Maui, *wishing* you had a nice, fine boyfriend...*always wishing* for what you're pushing a button to see. *Take note of this:* Your remote control won't make what you see on TV appear in real life.

Now let's say you decide to change your television habit. Essentially, there's nothing wrong with television—it's not a "one-eyed monster." The way you use it determines its value. Television can actually be very helpful. In fact, it could reward you. You could turn thirty cents an hour into a lot more if you watch the right programs.

It's a cause-and-effect relationship: News and weather channels are helpful anytime, or you could learn how to fix up your own home by watching these types of programs. Let's say you watch television for an hour and learn how to sand your hard-wood floors—you might be able to save $400–$1,000. That makes it worth your time! If you took recipe notes while watching a cooking program (to better care for your family), then it was worth your time. Television can be a benefit, but *be accountable*—always crunch the numbers.

The Discipline of Becoming Accountable

Begin to assess everything in your life and know why it happens. Then you'll be able to go back and correct mistakes (as long as you've taken everything into account). God will bless you for it. Make your soul accountable to Him. Psalm 34:8 says, "O taste and see that the Lord is good: blessed *is* the man *that* trusteth in Him." There's a level of accountability built into this passage. When you know *how* to *taste* and *see, how* to take note, then you'll be able to discern what trusting God *will produce.*

Let me take it a little further. I was raised with accountability. Whenever my father wanted to have something done, he always priced it out a minimum of three times. "Okay, the roof needs to be fixed…three bids." He'd negotiate, and sometimes it revealed the cheaper price wasn't necessarily the best price. And sometimes the highest price wasn't necessarily a bad price. Always count the cost.

This also reveals another level of accountability: We must always get details in writing. Several years ago, I started negotiating contracts for hotels and conferences. This is when I remembered something my father used to say, which was vital: "The salesperson you begin with today may not be there after today." There's a high turnover rate in hotel sales and marketing. So I'd negotiate a contract, sign it, and then we'd arrive and the *new* contacts weren't knowledgeable of the agreement.

For example, in 1995 I finished contract negotiations for *Praise Power Celebration* events until 2004. In the process of negotiating these contracts, I noticed many of the original signers were no longer with this organization, which left the arbitration of suite packages, rebates, cost analysis, free meeting space, additional bonuses and perks, and additional compensations to individual interpretation. It was as if the contract had been based on a handshake and *he said, she said*—but if you have it in writing, there's accountability.

Master the art of getting everything in writing. Become the businessperson that understands great communications skills. To help you in this process, check out the appendix at the end of the book. There's a list of great business books that address a number of important areas that will benefit you. These business resources will help you steer your spirit *and* your soul towards greater success and abundance.

It's Time to Turn

This takes me to an important turning point in my own understanding of accountability. In December 1997, I was preparing to pastor my church, and the Lord told me that He really wanted to sharpen some things in my life. So I went to a hotel in Washington, D.C., shut myself in, and read a book entitled, *The Instant Millionaire,* by Mark Fisher. After reading this book, some of my greatest weaknesses and strengths came to light.

Then the Lord asked me to count up as much debt as I could, and I ended up in a three-day shut-in, writing down every area of indebtedness. I didn't know that by the time I returned to Delaware, I'd get a telephone call from a person asking to meet with me to discuss "a couple of things" before I went to pastor. I sat down with this person who inquired, "Tell me how much debt you're in." And when I stated the figure, they paid off all of my debt because I already had accountability.

What would happen if someone came up to you today and said, "I want to pay off all your bills and make you debt free"? Would you know, exactly to the dollar, even to the penny, how much money you'd need to pay them off; or would you be scrambling for two or three weeks trying to get everything in full accountability (major credit card statements, gas bills, car payments, utilities, revolving credit card statements, student loans, personal loans, and so on)? Could you be readily accountable if God really wanted to make you debt free?

One of the books I highly recommend is entitled, *Ten Steps How To Get Debt Free,* by Bishop John Francis. This book will bless you, as well as his Web site (which appears on the back of his book). *If you really want to get debt free, then start living the Law of Accountability.* Start being accountable for the numbers.

After that, in 1997, I met my wife, Prophetess Juanita Bynum, for the first time. It was her first service at Praise Power Celebration in Baltimore, and as she began to prophesy, she grabbed me by the hand and said, "God said you're going to handle millions, millions, millions…" not knowing that I had written a soul prosperity decree. I was declaring on a daily basis,

"I am prospering, I have prospered, and I will continue to prosper…because it's God's will for me to prosper."

Many of you should write your own spiritual soul prosperity decree and declare it. No matter what the enemy says about your life, when you embrace accountability—when you focus on the numbers—God can take you to the next level. Get accountable for the things in your life, even down to how many times your children play Nintendo without studying; how many hours they're involved in *less* profitable activities; scheduling and being accountable for all of your time and resources. God wants to take you to another level.

There's another prophetic principle in Numbers that gives us a warning about negative accountability: When you become aware of who you are in God and all He's given you, don't fall into pride. Aaron and Miriam (Moses' brother and sister) spoke against Moses when he married an Ethiopian woman (Num. 12:1), "Hath the Lord indeed spoken only by Moses? hath he not spoken also by us? And the Lord heard it" (vs. 2). When we think too much of ourselves because of the blessings God has bestowed, He's obligated to set the record straight. Miriam was struck with leprosy and had to remain outside of the camp for seven days (see Num. 12:10–15).

Pride is deceptive, because by Numbers 16 a revolt was brought against Moses by Korah, Dathan, and Abiram—priests in the Levitical order. And they brought 250 leaders with them. "*Ye take* too much upon you, seeing all the congregation *are* holy, every one of them, and the Lord *is* among them: wherefore then lift ye up yourselves above the congregation of the Lord?" (Num.

16:3). *Now take note.* Each of these people knew exactly who they were and what their position in God afforded them. And they had counted every reason why they should be favored like Moses—only they'd forgotten...God is a God of order. So He caused the earth to swallow up the entire tribe of Korah along with their possessions (Num. 16:28–33). God made them accountable for what they'd done.

Never try to rise above your assignment. Let God lift you up (see James 4:10). And most of all, learn to count your blessings and give all the glory to God.

God's getting ready to lead you into divine increase. So let's bow our heads in prayer. "Lord, we worship You and thank You for the blessing of accountability. We thank You for teaching us how to become as responsible in our daily lives as we are in spending time with You. Help us to account for everything You've given us as You lead us into our destiny, in Jesus' name. Amen."

5

THE LAW OF INCREASE
AND OVERFLOW

*Now unto him that is able to do exceeding abundantly above
all that we ask or think, according to the power that worketh
in us,*

*Unto him be glory in the church by Christ Jesus throughout
all ages (Eph. 3:20–21).*

As we enter this final chapter of the *Torah of the Soul,* you
should now be able to recognize the rich blessings God
has bestowed upon you. You witnessed the creative abundance
of God in Genesis, where man became (and is becoming) a *living
soul.* Then you were expanded in Exodus by experiencing God
as I AM. In Leviticus, God brought you into the divine order of
discipline, and then He took you into Numbers to deal with
your accountability and integrity.

Now we've reached the fifth book, Deuteronomy, which
speaks of divine increase and overflow. It's where accountability
and integrity rise to a new level, because now God expects you
to walk in His commandments…*consistently*…until His image is

re-formed in you. Yes, throughout this entire process, God has been overshadowing you—until you come into complete *soul dominion* and possess your rightful inheritance.

The Greek word for *Deuteronomy* means "second lawgiving."[1] In other words, God's going to take you through what He's already taught you *a second time* in order to bring you into an overflow anointing. Remember: two is the number of *agreement* that releases divine power in the earth. It also proves you truly understand what God has taught you. It's like taking a test in school; you learn the material, and then you revisit it again sometime later to make sure you understand the principle. This is how you ultimately learn to access God on every level—by consistently identifying His voice within your soul and being obedient to Him, *even when it seems impossible.* In this respect, I compare Deuteronomy to *due diligence*—because Israel knew how to come out of bondage, they knew how to receive from God; *but now* they had to apply what God had taught them to possess the fullness of His promises.

The book of Deuteronomy is significant because Israel had to take many divine turns, geographically and in spiritual leadership, in order to reach Canaan. God had to start by eradicating fear, because moving to a new level of increase always involves new challenges and transitions. Israel had many enemies to overcome on their path to abundance, but God said, "Ye shall not fear them: for the Lord your God he shall fight for you" (Deut. 3:22).

So what's the prophetic principle? When God's leading you into a season of *increase,* you have to know that He's already gone before you. Then you will understand that you're already *more than a conqueror* (see Rom. 8:37). You only have to apply what He's already put within you.

Transitioning Into Wealth

Moses was the prophetic prototype in four of the first five chapters, the bearer of God's purpose from the Law of Expansion through the Law of Increase and Overflow. Yet remember, a new day (or era) in Scripture is usually marked by a change of leadership—like when Noah brought in a new season immediately after Adam died. And in order for the *new* to come, old things had to pass away.

It was time to lead a *renewed* people into a *new* day. And even though Moses prayed to enter the Promised Land, God wouldn't let him. "But charge Joshua, and encourage him, and strengthen him: for he shall go over before this people, and he shall cause them to inherit the land which thou shalt see" (Deut. 3:28).

How does this tie in to soul prosperity? Moses led a people who'd been blessed with abundance into discipline and accountability, *to make them rich in their souls*. The next generation followed Joshua into *wealth* across the Jordan in the Promised Land. Deuteronomy 8:18 says, "But thou shalt remember the Lord thy God: for *it is* he that giveth thee power to get wealth, that he may establish his covenant which he sware unto thy fathers, as *it is* this day." So, *rich* applies to individual growth, but *wealth* transforms a nation.

Now let's look at it from the practical side. Being rich reflects a spirit of discipline as one looks at "little" and sees the value of maintaining and managing it. In other words, I start small, but what I have in my soul is making me rich. It's part of the spirit of increase. Wealth deals with major acquisitions that are of long-term value. General ups and downs in the stock market won't deplete them. This includes land, assets, securities, bonds, funds liquidity, and so on.

The power to get wealth is generated on the networking (or national) level. A nation doesn't become rich; it acquires wealth. A *person* becomes rich. Rich focuses in one area of worth, value, and abundance. Wealth must be generated by a collective effort on multiple levels. It involves tapping your resources and utilizing them to their fullest potential. If God's going to give you the power to get wealth, it will have to be through networking amongst people with extraordinary vision, establishing diverse relationships, and building collective power or ability to increase beyond individual effort.

In Deuteronomy, Israel comes out of selfish and sinful worship and begins to focus on their eternal covenant with God. During this time, the expression of integrity moved from personal to corporate—establishing, referencing, and reverencing the anointing of a national covenant. So in this respect, God began to move Israel into collective wealth by re-focusing them on what He'd said in the past. "So shall my word be that goeth forth out of my mouth: it shall not return unto me void, but it shall accomplish that which I please, and it shall prosper *in the thing* whereto I sent it" (Isa. 55:11).

God challenged Israel with a promise: "For if ye shall diligently keep all these commandments which I command you, to
do them, to love the Lord your God, to walk in all his ways, and
to cleave unto him; Then will the Lord drive out all these nations
from before you, and ye shall possess greater nations and mightier than yourselves" (Deut. 11:22–23).

Here's a powerful prophetic principle: A generational blessing is always released when you respect a covenant. And God
will drive fear, intimidation, and weakness far away from you.
When you operate in covenant, you know from your own
actions that you're not alone. Others will protect your interests,
just like you protect theirs. Covenant people don't have to focus
on themselves. And if you do, *hear this.* God's not going to grant
a generational blessing to people who simply look out for
number one.

Rising to the Generational Blessing

Deuteronomy 11:26–28 continues, "Behold, I set before you
this day a blessing and a curse; A blessing, if ye obey the commandments of the Lord your God, which I command you this
day: And a curse, if ye will not obey the commandments of the
Lord your God, but turn aside out of the way which I command
you this day, to go after other gods, which ye have not known."

A crucial law is at work here that touches three specific
areas: *hearing, obeying,* and *diligently pursuing.* In other words, I
hear God, obey Him, and diligently pursue exactly what He's
revealed for me to do—because I truly understand (by experience) that I'll either be blessed or cursed by my decision.

Therefore, my soul chooses to obey. This is how you come to maturity and are able to inherit all that God has for you.

I believe this is why many believers today are deadlocked in the area of financial prosperity—we haven't diligently kept ALL the commandments of the Lord. We haven't layered them in our spirits so that God can thrust us into the next level of corporate responsibility and wealth. Instead, we pick and choose what we'll obey...and lose the opportunity to prosper *even as* He deepens the prosperity of our inner man.

This brings me to another point from Deuteronomy 11:29. "And it shall come to pass, when the Lord thy God hath brought thee in unto the land whither thou goest to possess it, that thou shalt put the blessing upon mount Gerizim, and the curse upon mount Ebal." In other words, you can't mix blessings and curses. This is a vital part of maturity, because before you can enter into a covenant relationship with God, you have to let go of anything that could potentially separate you from Him. Otherwise, mixed emotions will defile you, and your faith will be locked in a mortal battle against fear.

If you're going to move forward in God, faith and fear must be permanently separated. Obedience must go on one side, and disobedience on the other. You cannot allow them to mix, or you could abort your heavenly blessings. You must *hear, obey,* and *diligently pursue* if you want to receive anything from God. "For he that wavereth is like a wave of the sea driven with the wind and tossed. For let not that man think that he shall receive any thing of the Lord" (James 1:6–7).

The Voice of the Inner Prophet

This leads me into something that I call the *prophet of your soul*—because every true believer has it. "For as many as are led by the Spirit of God, they are the sons of God. The Spirit itself beareth witness with our spirit, that we are the children of God" (Rom. 8:14,16). This same spirit, the *Holy Spirit,* "shall teach you all things, and bring all things to your remembrance, whatsoever I have said unto you. For the testimony of Jesus is the spirit of prophecy" (John 14:26; Rev. 19:10).

If you're a child of God, you have an inner prophet (a *second voice* of God or another way in which He speaks to you)—and if you're honest, you can identify when you've heard His voice. Your soul can hear from your spirit, the epicenter, the place where God can speak to you clearly, if you let Him. He'll come forward, *resonate,* through the spirit of prophecy. On the other hand, a false prophet can also rise up within your soul, if you relinquish your spiritual dominion by walking according to the flesh instead of the Spirit. Everyone has an inner prophet—from the Spirit or from the flesh—and the voice you yield to will assume control.

God warned Israel in Deuteronomy 13:1-4:

> *If there arise among you a prophet, or a dreamer of dreams, and giveth thee a sign or a wonder, And the sign or the wonder come to pass, whereof he spake unto thee, saying, Let us go after other gods, which thou hast not known, and let us serve them; Thou shalt not hearken unto the words of that prophet, or that dreamer of dreams: for the Lord your God proveth you, to know whether ye love the Lord your God with all your heart and with all your soul. Ye shall walk after the Lord your God, and fear him, and keep his commandments, and*

obey his voice, and ye shall serve him, and cleave unto him (emphasis mine).

Your inner prophet—the voice of the Lord through the Holy Spirit—always leads you to obedience. He quickens you to fear the Lord, because when you fear God, you obviously have faith in him: "…that he is, and *that* he is a rewarder of them that diligently seek him" (Heb. 11:6). So when challenges come, follow your inner voice that tells you to bless the Lord instead of giving up; bless His name instead of believing He's forsaken you. Cleave unto God, and you'll extinguish the lies of the enemy of your soul.

This is the process you must endure to possess your divine inheritance. "And the prophet, or that dreamer of dreams, shall be put to death; *because he hath spoken to turn you away from the Lord your God,* which brought you out of the land of Egypt, and redeemed you out of the house of bondage, to thrust thee out of the way which the Lord thy God commanded thee to walk in. *So shalt thou put the evil away from the midst of thee*" (Deut. 13:5, *emphasis mine*).

By putting to death the false prophet in your soul, you regain soul dominion. And when you've taken possession of your most precious gift, God will entrust you with more. *Do you see the prophetic principle?* God expects us to regain dominion of our own souls before He'll trust us with corporate responsibility—no matter how many twists and turns we have to take. So when your soul tries to shut down (from hearing the lies of the enemy), your new man must rise up and declare, "Why art thou cast down, O my soul? and *why* art thou disquieted in me? hope thou in God: for I shall yet praise him *for* the help of his countenance" (Ps. 42:5).

Keep your soul in the right environment by staying in the presence of God, and the inner false prophet will die.

The Turning of My Soul

In 1996, I found myself at a crossroads. I'd been living in Wilmington, Delaware, for over fifteen years and was President of the District Young People for the Washington, D.C., Delaware, and Maryland region. One day on my way to a District Council meeting, I traveled to D.C. on the Amtrak train and then had to wait for an hour outside of Union Station. That hour was significant. God began to attune me to the atmosphere of the city. As I stood at Union Station, it strangely began to feel like home...so much so that I felt as if I could be home in a few moments, somewhere in that city.

Shortly after I returned to Wilmington that evening, I started to sense another shift—like I was just visiting. God had taken a turn in my life, and I knew it. I couldn't explain it, didn't know all of the details, but in my soul *something had changed*. I couldn't deny it.

Every believer is built to recognize when God's about to do something distinctive and mighty in his or her life. There's a sudden shifting...one moment you have one focus, and the next moment everything's different. And then God says, "Ye have dwelt long enough in this mount: Turn you, and take your journey, and go" (Deut. 1:6–7). Little did I know, God was moving me to the next level of covenant responsibility. And there were many nations, "greater and mightier" than I was, that I'd have to encounter one day.

In the Beginning...

I acknowledged to my father that I was called to pastor in Washington, D.C. It turned out to be one of the most ambitious endeavors I'd ever taken. I did have the advantage of helping my father start his church years before, so I knew what it took to birth a work from scratch. I knew I couldn't take anything for granted.

In 1996–97, I began to pray for God to reveal His will concerning acquiring a building in Washington, D.C. As I prayed, God told me to seek out the land. So I went to Washington and began to look, driving around and seeing the various levels of poverty, status, and potential in the city.

During my prayer time, the Lord told me to contact a realtor with whom I'd become acquainted by word of mouth. Soon after, he was helping me in my search. Another congregation was temporarily renting the first building while they built their new facility. So I was considering renting the building to start my services on days they didn't meet. Of course, my proposal was rejected.

Then I noticed there was a school next door on Ridge Road. Not long after (back in Wilmington), I'd finished praying at my office, and the Lord said, "Call the school on Ridge Road." When I called to get the number, the operator gave me the number of another school that was a half-mile up the street from the one I wanted to contact...and soon, I received a new revelation. Little did I know, my inner prophet was already guiding me.

Expanding My Borders

I called the school and asked if there was space available for rent. The person told me, "Yes," so I inquired about the process. I was told I had to contact the school district to request a time...and then I hung up the phone. The Lord spoke to me again, "Call back and ask for the principal."

I immediately went into a debate with God. "Why do you want me to call back? I've found out they have space. I found out how to go about it. I got the number!"

The Lord said again, "Call back and ask for the principal."

I called and asked to speak with the principal. When I did, the person began to tell me that the principal was overwhelmed because the night before it had been confirmed the school would be closing indefinitely. I said, "Okay," and hung up. That was my signal.

Deuteronomy 18:15,21-22 says:

The Lord thy God will raise up unto thee a Prophet from the midst of thee, of thy brethren, like unto me; unto him ye shall hearken. And if thou say in thine heart, How shall we know the word which the Lord hath not spoken? When a prophet speaketh in the name of the Lord, if the thing follow not, nor come to pass, that is the thing which the Lord hath not spoken, but the prophet hath spoken it presumptuously: thou shalt not be afraid of him.

Don't be afraid of a false prophet, in or outside of your soul, because the Lord will not honor that false report! Listen. I had two prophets working in me that day—*but I knew the voice of my Lord. And I obeyed Him.* Never listen to the voice of doubt in your soul.

Deuteronomy 18:19 says, "And it shall come to pass, *that* whosoever will not hearken unto my words which he shall speak in my name, I will require *it* of him." This means that we have to watch out for soul turns. Times when our souls are anguished, frustrated, bewildered—when we're facing a crisis or challenge—and our soul gets uprooted from the passion of our purpose. Sometimes all it takes is a little shift, and the passion is gone.

I could have turned the wrong direction that day; if I had followed the false prophet, like my body wanted to, I would have put the call off until later. After all, I was tired. Still, my soul stirred when I heard the voice of God. *Let me encourage you*—never follow your senses over the voice of the Holy Spirit. That's what animals do because they haven't been given the *breath of life.* They sniff the ground for direction. You are far above that. You're a *living soul,* a child of the eternal God.

I went to see the school because now *I knew* it was being closed—but the real significance hit me when it aired on the 11:30 news that night. I had prayed that morning, "Lord, give me clarity on Your will." Everything became crystal clear. So I immediately began to pursue what I knew had been my Father's voice.

The next morning (in early June 1997), I left for Washington and drove to the school with my camcorder. I walked through and taped everything I could. I met several people there. I walked in the hallways with the decree of the Lord in my mouth concerning that property. It had 54,000 square feet, twenty-two classrooms, a playground, a baseball/football field, a 200-seat auditorium, a separate dining area (off of the auditorium), office space, and ample parking—all on a major road in the city.

Coming Into Divine Order

I immediately recognized that the Lord was giving me an incredible opportunity. However, I didn't immediately respond to fulfill the entire process. A dark cloud seemed to be forming, which started to block my vision. It seemed the more I shared with friends, the more they didn't bear witness with where God was taking me. The voice of my inner prophet got weaker and weaker; and before long, I was experiencing full-blown fear.

The false prophet reminded me...*here I was,* coming through a major separation and financial stripping. And at the same time, I was undergoing a dramatic turn in my ministry. The voice of condemnation could have stopped me, but the Lord kept reminding me, He could still pour everything out to me that I needed to fulfill my destiny. God was rebuilding me, making me sensitive to the needs of hurting people. All the while I was decreeing unto God in the midst of an intense struggle.

I had been going through an extremely hard time in my life, and in that two years, God tested my commitment to His will. During this process I lost all five of my vehicles...and it came to the point that, for one year, I walked back and forth to the church. I'd been evicted from my apartment due to the financial struggle. And if that wasn't enough, while working toward getting the church from Wilmington, Delaware, all of my Platinum American Express and Gold Cards were either going defunct or into collections. I'd also gone through a major setback where companies garnished my check for loans that had to be paid. After tithes and offerings, I ended up receiving only $6.40 per week for myself. Six dollars and forty cents! My dad even told me that it didn't make sense how I was able to live.

No one invited me to preach. Every door closed. It was devastating—absolutely the worst experience of my life. Friends stopped calling me, wouldn't even associate with me. And my enemies loved to see me being destroyed. Many of them cursed the fact that I even called myself *blessed* in the midst of this situation.

I went through the process of *overshadowing*. I was stripped of everything, so that I could learn to give all of my praises to God. My relationship with Him became vital. Jesus became the cornerstone of my existence. *And that's when the Lord took me to Isaiah 11:1-2 [inserts mine]:* "And there shall come forth a rod out of the stem of Jesse, and a Branch shall grow out of his roots: And the spirit of the Lord [1] shall rest upon him, [2] the spirit of wisdom and [3] understanding, [4] the spirit of counsel and [5] might, [6] the spirit of knowledge and of [7] the fear of the Lord." I took hold of it, and it changed my life. Now I know that when my enemy comes, these seven things equip me to walk in the fullness of my anointing. My enemy actually brings me exponential increase in the mind of God.

First of all, I understand what the Spirit is decreeing to me about the church...my soul understands my eternal destiny. And when the Lord speaks, I can rest in Him. Second, the Spirit gives me wisdom by revealing what I need to do. Third, He gives me understanding by revealing how I should do what He commands. Fourth, He blesses me with supernatural counsel and confirms the path I am to follow. Fifth, the spirit of might guards my soul and assures me that I'm more than a conqueror. And sixth, the spirit of knowledge gives me specific insight in every situation. Last but not least, the fear of the Lord keeps me from letting the enemy have any place in my life.

These seven ingredients remind me of orange juice—rich in Vitamin C, but fortified with other good vitamins. So the Spirit of Truth is the key element in this process, but the other ingredients fulfill the process of edifying your soul. And now I truly understand Christ as *the stem out of Jesse*...because from the root of divine relationship with Him, I'm watered by divine purpose, connection, and impartation. Jesus is the divine Branch of nourishment for every tree that He plants by rivers of water (see Ps. 1:3). I have learned that even in the dead of winter, I can bear fruits of faith and righteousness unto Christ. I have learned that if I keep my eyes on Jesus and delight in His law, He'll bring me out of midnight into a new day.

Now watch this because it's a powerful tie-in. Deuteronomy 28:1-2,7 *(emphasis mine)* says:

> *And it shall come to pass, if thou shalt hearken diligently unto the voice of the Lord thy God, to observe and to do all his commandments which I command thee this day... all*

these blessings shall come on thee, and overtake thee, if thou shalt hearken unto the voice of the Lord thy God. The Lord shall cause thine enemies that rise up against thee to be smitten before thy face: they shall come out against thee one way, and flee before thee seven ways.

Here's a prophetic principle: Your enemy can't flee from you seven ways until you fulfill the seven requirements of Isaiah 11. That's also why the enemy comes back with seven more spirits "more wicked than himself" once you've set your house in order (see Luke 11:26)—*because he knows he has to attack you in an area that's already been perfected.*

Once I got my "roots" in place, I began writing the vision God had given me for three companies. Now let me say that while I was writing this plan (utilizing the entrepreneurial anointing that was on my life), I was still walking to church with holes in the bottoms of my shoes (so when it rained I'd actually have to lead the worship service with soaking feet)...I couldn't even bow down to pray without the holes in my shoes being exposed...and I couldn't tell people that all I had in my refrigerator for a whole week was one gallon of water. *Anything,* a simple candy bar or a bag of potato chips, was a delight. *Yet all of these things developed the decree of the Lord in my soul.*

Let me encourage you. Never be discouraged about your present situation when God's beginning to give you a prophetic word—because when He tells you that you're going to come out and increase, you'll come out with more than you've ever had...more than you've ever known.

Yes, it was a struggle to look at someone driving a Mercedes Benz when I had to walk, but I learned how to celebrate Him, and that was worth it all. *Learn how to celebrate His sovereignty.* It will literally carry you through any trial, because His wisdom always leads to greater glory and victory.

The Process of Accountability

Slowly, I resumed my pursuit of the property and began to write a proposal. After I submitted it, they placed an ad in a local newspaper (as they'd told me) for any other parties that might be interested. This was around August. For some reason, I was afraid to use the power of being first to know about the opportunity. *This reveals a prophetic principle:* As God leads you into soul prosperity, He'll present you with an opportunity to move on something *first.* So, although I actually finished writing the proposal in July, I didn't submit it until August—*because I didn't see any money.*

Opportunity comes to everyone but waits for no one. Soul prosperity begins with obedience. *I recognized that I had to obey the opportunity God was giving me in order to seize the moment.* Interestingly, as I recalled the vision, I realized the reason God had caused me to call the school building down the street. The first church I had seen was actually too small to house my vision! My vision was much larger than 10,000 square feet. God knew I needed at least 40,000 more.

Let me review. The spirit of the Lord spoke to me that morning in June so that I'd go check out the building. Then the spirit of wisdom began to give me clarity about the plan. The spirit of understanding allowed me to do what was necessary to complete this part of the vision. So then I began to pursue the financial area, and I was fearful because I didn't have any resources. *I had to walk in soul prosperity.* I had to see myself always prospering in the things of the Lord, because I had the ability to foresee what God was going to do. I saw the spiritual reality through the window of my soul, in faith, because my soul was prospering in the Lord.

As the application process continued, several others made bids on the property. In fact, I was getting a little weary because the District of Columbia moved so slowly, it frustrated my timetable to open the church as it was. On October 6 that year, I opened prayer services at a hotel in Washington. Then about a month later, my father, Bishop Thomas Wesley Weeks, Sr., visited the area and I took him to the building. It was all boarded up. Broken glass, overgrown weeds everywhere, torn down fences…the building was in a state of decay and abandonment. In fact, someone had driven a car into the lot and set it on fire right next to the building. I thank God that only a small portion was damaged.

My father, a business graduate who also understood property values, walked the grounds with me. I couldn't get into the building because I didn't have any keys. In my spirit, though, I already knew that God had spoken to me to propose an offer of one million dollars. After my father walked around the parking lot, playground, and other areas, he returned to the car and said, "You know, if I was making an offer for this particular building, for what I know you could do with it, I'd offer them a million dollars." Without saying a word, I got in the car, and we drove back to the church.

You see, that's where the spirit of counsel comes in. I'm talking about somebody who has already walked down the avenue you're traveling and you know is seasoned to give you the right information—not biased or skewed—but something that echoes what God has been saying in the prophet of your soul. Counsel reveals a *true prophet* to recognize divine potential.

My father would admit to you that he thought I was crazy...knowing my financial condition, knowing that my paycheck was being garnished, knowing that I only had $6.40 to live on every week after tithes and offerings. However, even in the midst of doors slamming shut, God caused me to trust in the Spirit that was resting upon me. And in November, while I was coming through this, they sent my proposal to the Emergency Control Board in Washington, D.C. At the time, I was also looking for other locations, just in case the approval process took a bit longer.

Then I ran into a realtor who was very astute about church property. In fact, about 80 percent of the top churches in the D.C. metropolitan area had some interaction with him. So, without letting him know I'd bid on it, I asked discreetly, "What do you think about the school building on Ridge Road?" He thought it had already been purchased. "I know three companies that have bid on it, and they all have the money to pay for it in cash; so it's sold already."

To tell you the truth, I'd already resigned to the fact that I wasn't going to get the building. If three companies who had the ability to pay for it in cash had put in proposals, who was I to bid with only a word in my soul? *I just knew the building was gone.* Then a few days later (the week before Thanksgiving), the board took the proposal and began to dialogue about it. That Monday night, I asked a few intercessors (who had been attending our prayer services) to go into intercession. By Thursday night, we were getting ready for the dialogue.

At the meeting, I was told that *seven* companies had submitted bids, and three had said they could pay cash. I had made the first bid but didn't have any money to do it. So I lifted it up to God. "If this is Your will, Lord, You've got to produce it." And that's when the spirit of might came upon me. I began to confess it, to decree that in spite of what I'd been told—there was another way, another opportunity, another potential buyer, or another situation—*I could press through it.* The truth of the matter is, God gave me the ability to see myself as victorious by walking in the spirit of might.

That evening (after I'd fasted in agreement with others), the board came back and said, "We have selected the vision of [at that time] Pastor Weeks." It was really Reverend Weeks, because my entrepreneurial business savvy was to present my vision as the leader in an organizational trilogy called the Center of Hope Ministries, the Center of Hope Community Development Corporation, and the Center of Hope Enterprises. They approved the vision that I'd presented, versus those by the companies with "big" deals and cold cash!

The Lord reminded me of Deuteronomy 7:1 (*emphasis mine*), "When the Lord thy God shall bring thee into the land whither thou goest to possess it, and hath cast out many nations before thee...*seven nations* greater and mightier than thou...." Hallelujah! God had perfected my journey and confirmed again that I was walking in His path to abundance.

When God gives you a word, move on it! Go and possess the land! Don't let money make you hesitate on whatever He's decreed for you. Don't let the people around you make you hesitate, because the Word of the Lord is true! "...he which hath begun a good work in you will perform it..." (Phil. 1:6). He's able to bring it to pass, make it happen—*birth it out*—see it completed! He's able to make sure it is "exceeding abundantly above" all you could ask or think (Eph. 3:20).

Yes, there were times that the enemy tried to come back and fight the spirit of might that was flowing within me...but I had to hold on to the fact that I'd *hearkened diligently* unto the voice of the Lord. I had gone through the process of the *Torah of the Soul*, and I knew I was creating the law of seeing God's vision come to pass.

A New Day of Divine Increase

I absolutely knew that God was expanding me beyond my horizons. The new building was almost three times as big as the church I was leaving. And He was also bringing me into a level of divine order, into the vision of my mind. From childhood, I was always creative. I always wanted more, did more, pursued more; I didn't let anything hold me back...and it brought me into the divine order of pursuing the character of the anointing that was on my life.

Also, in the midst of this journey, God was beginning to birth another level of accountability in me, where I had to follow through on a new level of relationships, dialogue, and networking. It wasn't difficult, but entirely new, because there were new people and new arenas to learn. After that, I began to experience the spirit of knowledge to implement the plan in order of priority.

The spirit of knowledge gave me steps to complete the process. To get the idea of how to accomplish it, I had to sit around people that had done it before. I didn't have knowledge of how to run a 54,000 square foot complex in my back pocket. So I had to gain knowledge on various levels of skill to add security, staff, and engineers for the building. When I first walked through the building, I knew how much it would probably cost, because the boiler in my father's church was about one-fourth the size of just *one* of the boilers in this building. Using a small litmus test, this meant it would be eight times more expensive to run than my former church. *That one little glimpse taught me a lot about management and what needed to take place for God to work in my favor.*

Now let's go back and revisit something. After I was approved for the building in December, I still had a problem; so I did the three-day shut-in at the hotel in Washington, D.C. That's when I read *The Instant Millionaire* and God moved miraculously to pay off my debt. It was one (major!) thing that the debt was paid for; but it was also one of many signs that confirmed God was giving me favor to pastor and to come into the pastorate *debt free.* Yet, I still had to overcome some personal dilemmas.

Let me encourage you. If you're currently facing a dilemma or your life is dysfunctional, it's because God is testing whether or not you'll let that thing control you. I was about to give up the prophetic word inside me, until it brought me to an important realization. *Whatever stops you from your soul prosperity and destiny becomes your god.* So I learned to let some things go and let God be God. The prophet of your soul will reveal God's plan for you.

So I went from having nothing to being debt free by the twenty-fifth of December that year. Then at a watch-night service on December 31, my public transition came…and I walked away from seventeen years of history and investment. When I pulled up to the church, the Lord spoke to me, "I know you're not feeling like you want to leave; I know you're feeling like you don't want to go pastor….but you've been faithful and obedient."

My father laid his hands on me and blessed my new assignment and full-time pastorate, which caused a *supernatural flow* into my life. After the service, a person came up to me with a check for $3,000. He didn't know that I needed $2,900 to pay for insurance on the building and parts for the engineers to get the boiler started, among other things. Once again, God granted me *soul prosperity* because I had obeyed His voice.

Even As Your Soul Prospers

Before we move into the next section, I want to emphasize that when God speaks a "soul word" to you regarding your destiny, you must come into complete alignment with His vision. And you must call it what God has named it…and maintain the proper focus, because this path will lead you into *soul* expansion. You'll find that as you begin to walk the path to true abundance, a 25/40 vision or a 3x5 mind just won't cut it. God's vision is too big. You must learn to rest in His shadow and let Him guide you.

Remember that you've been created in the *image* and *likeness* of God as spirit, soul, and body. Keep your spirit conscious of God, your soul aware of what He's calling you to do, and your body cognizant of the world around you. God's in the process of revealing *to you* who you really are; He's trying to help you find your purpose.

He's also going to bring you into divine order. And you'll begin to have charge over your house, as well as your soul. *God will see to it that the anointing on your life begins to fall into accountability,* and that you'll learn what's necessary to prove your areas of strength. God's birthing something inside of you. He's shaping a new image that will continue to sharpen into spiritual integrity and divine increase. You will learn to hearken diligently unto the Lord from the prophet of your soul, because it's been echoing into your being everything God wants you to accomplish.

I decree that just as you've finished this portion of the book, you'll also come into agreement with God about your own soul prosperity. You can never prosper abundantly trying to identify with someone else's greatness and ignoring *your* assignment. I decree that the Spirit of the Lord will come upon you with wisdom, understanding, counsel, might, knowledge, and the fear of the Lord. *You shall walk in the power of your soul prosperity.* Amen.

PART 2

THE PROSPERITY
OF THE SOUL—
RELEASE YOUR BLESSINGS

6

LET NOT THE LAW DEPART OUT OF THY MOUTH

Blessed is the man that walketh not in the counsel of the ungodly, nor standeth in the way of sinners, nor sitteth in the seat of the scornful.

But his delight is in the law of the Lord; and in his law doth he meditate day and night.

…whatsoever he doeth shall prosper (Ps. 1:1-3).

When Moses died, his death marked the beginning of a new season of destiny. And God re-established the principle of soul dominion by setting in a new leader, who would take Israel across the Jordan River into the Promised Land. (Years later, the prophet John the Baptist would baptize Jesus of Nazareth in this same river to begin a new kingdom order.)

Moses had completed everything God commanded him to do and prophetically established the *Torah of the Soul*. "Come now therefore, and I will send thee unto Pharaoh, that thou mayest bring forth my people the children of Israel out of Egypt. And he said, Certainly I will be with thee; and this shall be a token unto thee, that I have sent thee: When thou hast brought forth the people out of Egypt, ye shall serve God upon this mountain" (Ex. 3:10,12). From the beginning, Moses knew Israel was destined to go into Canaan, *but first,* he had to obey God's commands and teach them how to prosper in their souls. "But seek ye first the kingdom of God, and his righteousness; and *all these things* shall be *added unto you*" (Matt. 6:33, *emphasis mine*).

Now it was time to build the wealth of the nation...and only two from the first generation were allowed to make this transition: Joshua and Caleb. So in the new day, God chose Joshua to become the new prophetic prototype for the next level of soul prosperity—corporate wealth and abundance. It was as if God was saying to Joshua, "Well done, good and faithful servant; thou hast been faithful over a few things, I will make thee ruler over many things: enter thou into the joy of thy lord" (Matt. 25:23).

Deuteronomy 34:9 says, "And Joshua the son of Nun was full of the spirit of wisdom; for Moses had laid his hands upon him: and the children of Israel hearkened unto him, and did as the Lord commanded Moses." Moses walked with God, and Joshua walked with Moses. This is why Joshua received the new assignment. You see, when God's overshadowing process is complete, you come out filled with His wisdom—and that's when you're ready to declare the Word of the Lord.

The book of Proverbs says, "The tongue of the wise useth knowledge aright: but the mouth of fools poureth out foolishness. The prosperity of fools shall destroy them" (15:2; 1:32). In other words, God's not going to call you into leadership until He knows you've gained the wisdom to speak life into darkness, until you've learned to create the same atmosphere that He spoke into existence at the beginning of time. James 3:2 says, "If any man offend not in word, the same is a perfect man, and able also to bridle the whole body." Joshua's faith had been perfected, so he rose to a corporate anointing. He was given charge over the entire nation of Israel.

Blessed is the person that God overshadows: and in His shadow learns not to walk in ungodly counsel, and not to think he's better than anyone else, and to seek God first in everything. This person delights in God day and night. And this person, who is rich in soul, is able to possess wealth. This person is planted by "rivers of water," and bears fruit—summer, spring, winter, and fall. And in the new generation of Israelites, Joshua was that person. When he led them into Canaan, prosperity wouldn't destroy them. *Whatsoever* Joshua did as unto the Lord would prosper.

The Call to a New Day

God said to Joshua, "Moses my servant is dead; now therefore arise, go over this Jordan, thou, and all this people....Every place that the sole of your foot shall tread upon, that have I given unto you, as I said unto Moses" (Josh. 1:2–3). Now Joshua already knew Moses was dead, but God had to tell him again because Joshua had to change his posture. In other words, Joshua was *sitting, laid back,* and *timid.* He was still postured to wait for Moses' command. That's why God told Joshua to *arise.*

It's like God was saying, "Listen, Joshua, Moses isn't coming back. And since there's a chance that you'll think I may resurrect him—since you know I gave Moses power to do awesome wonders—I'm confirming to you that he's gone. Yes, Moses walked with me and had soul prosperity. Resurrection power lived inside of him because Moses believed that I AM. Now, Joshua, it's your turn. I want you to walk with Me like you saw Moses do, because I have a job for you to accomplish."

Joshua faced a dilemma. He had served as Moses' assistant for many years. He had been on Mount Sinai with Moses for forty days and nights (see Ex. 24:13–18). He had heard "a noise of war in the camp" as they came down the mountain (Ex. 32:15–17). Joshua and Caleb were sent to spy out the land and were the only two (out of twelve) that came back with a good report. "If the Lord delight in us, then he will bring us into this land, and give it us; a land which floweth with milk and honey" (Num. 14:8). Joshua knew that God spoke to Moses face to face.

Let me explain. Some of us get stuck thinking that only one person can minister to us, give us the Word of the Lord, or issue the charge to go forward. So the Lord repeated, "Moses isn't going to come back, so you need to arise and get ready to do what you've been ordained, prepared, and assigned to do. Arise and do what you've already seen Moses do…go over this Jordan. And make sure you go over with the same purpose and passion you had the first time."

God wanted Joshua to begin declaring what he'd already seen. So He let him know it was his season of increase. And He'll do the same for you. You see, sometimes God has to pull you aside and tell you when something is dead. No matter how badly you want it to come back, when God says it's dead, *it's gone*. You have to learn how to let dead things go and enter a new day.

Here's a prophetic principle: If you're going to possess what God has promised, you have to *see it* and then *say it,* in order to *receive it.* God had already given Joshua the vision to possess the land; now He was challenging him to possess it.

A lot of people try to *name it* and *claim it,* but the problem comes when they're not saying what God has revealed in their spirit and what they have received by their soul. As a result, the soul doesn't prosper, so what they've been naming and claiming does not come to pass. From the beginning, God established Adam's dominion authority through the power of his voice. Every part of creation was as subject to Adam's voice as it was to the voice of God, until Adam fell into sin. When Adam withheld the words of God in the Garden, he lost everything—he lost soul dominion (see Gen. 3:6). Without the Word of God being heard in the spirit and received in the soul, our words are void of the power and purpose of God.

The Power of Divine Agreement

Joshua stood at the dawn of a new era, and God was challenging him to rise up and take dominion authority. It would be Joshua's second time to cross the Jordan—*the number of divine agreement*—so it was a prophetic symbol that something powerful was going to be released. *Listen to me.* Don't hesitate when God gives you a commandment, *especially* when He's allowed you to see your destiny before it happens. Let's say God gives you the opportunity to sit at a desk that could be your next promotion. Don't act like you're not supposed to sit there if He's already allowed you to *taste* and *see!* It's time for you to possess it!

When I test-drive a car, I believe it's already mine. I don't care what the sticker price is, or what I have to do to get it financed; *it's already done.* Once I sit in the car, I already believe it belongs to me. You see, I'm one of those crazy people that test drives a car and stops to fill the tank (most cars that I've test driven are almost empty, to the point the indicator light's almost glowing). When I get in, I tell the salesman to let me stop at a gas station and fill it up—just like it's my car. And while I'm holding the pump I say, "God, I thank You the payment is being made, I thank You for making the way, I thank You for opening the door...." In doing so, I'm declaring to Him, "I'm going to arise and cross over into this blessing that You've given me."

I went into a house in Philadelphia once that was selling for $275,000. It was brand new—decorated in art deco—in the yuppie section of downtown Green Street, across from a famous French restaurant. Everything I'd prayed for in my previous house, I asked God to give me in this house: hardwood floors throughout, a special master bedroom, two fireplaces, a three-car garage, and a Jacuzzi with a matching fireplace (together in one area). I laid it out before God in separate zones.

When the realtor walked me through the house, I took dominion. I activated the vision and expanded into my destiny. I knew this was my time to possess the land. I'd already come into divine order and accounted for the numbers, so when I went into *that* land, I was bold and courageous. I treated it like it was already mine. I excused myself to go to the restroom— and by the time I came downstairs, the realtor said she'd just gotten a call from the owner and the price of the house had dropped $100,000.

Here's the prophetic principle: You have to arise in God in order to accomplish what other people think is impossible. When God knows you have enough faith, He'll bring your blessing to you…*wherever you are.* You see, the initial price kept other people from buying the house before I got there, but when I stepped into it, God said, "I'll move whatever I have to move to get you in." This is what God was saying to Joshua: "Go forth over this Jordan, because you've already put your footprints in the river. I know that I can trust you, Joshua, because you already have soil between your toes. You've already seen what's on the other side."

God's Test of Leadership

I believe the reason God can't bless many believers is that we're not willing to go over the Jordan alone. We're not willing to be the first one over. We want others to touch, agree, and believe God with us—and that's fine, because there's power in agreement. It doesn't replace, however, the fact that each one of us is required to hear, obey, and diligently pursue our own assignment. Are you willing to hear His command and *Go?* Will you arise in the prosperity of your soul and become a leader?

God told Joshua, "I'm going to transfer everything your feet touch…everything the soles of your feet land on…into your possession. I'm going to give you what I promised Moses. I didn't stop the promise when Moses died…I'm going to transfer what I promised Moses into your hands." *Say this right now—* "I'm ready for a transfer." *Declare it to God,* "I'm ready for something to be spoken into my life that will make my soul leap, celebrate, and magnify You."

God can bless you beyond what you're able to imagine and take you into new realms of prosperity. He'll say, "You know that house that you saw with Mary? I'm going to give you a house just like that. You didn't know why you were walking through that four-bedroom house with a three-car garage, but I wanted you to see it. She had the faith for it, but I had to get you to the place where you desired it, so that you'd have a point of reference when I told you to possess what I have for you."

Let's say you go across town to deliver a package. Then you realize, "Hey, I'd like to work on *that* side of town." You hadn't seen that side of town, but the package gave you the opportunity to desire it. God will cause strange things to happen by allowing something to get into your spirit that you can't shake. Why? *Your soul knows your next level.* That's why God begins to transfer things to you when you don't even think they're yours.

Now let me ask you a few things. Do you believe that you can do even greater things than Jesus did? Do you believe God can use you to teach others about Him, heal the sick, cast out demons, or speak in heavenly languages? Do you believe that you can come through *whatsoever* is testing your faith right now?

Do you think, "Jesus was able to do that; I can't" or "Jesus had that authority; I don't"? *Here's a prophetic principle:* Jesus walked with God. If you walk with Jesus, you can rise up in the prosperity of your soul, activate these same promises, and possess true wealth and abundance (see John 14:12; Mark 16:15–18; Matt. 17:20).

Are You in the Place of Your Assignment?

Let's return to Joshua. God was confirming to him, "My Word won't return unto Me void because Moses is dead. My Word is alive. Moses passed away, but My Word is still living and active in the earth. My Word can still change the atmosphere; all you have to do is receive My Word and you'll pick up where Moses left off. You'll be able to know what I'm going to do in the earth and walk in it." This raises the issue of location.

"From the wilderness and this Lebanon even unto the great river, the river Euphrates, all the land of the Hittites, and unto the great sea toward the going down of the sun, shall be your coast. There shall not any man be able to stand before thee all the days of thy life: as I was with Moses, so I will be with thee: I will not fail thee, nor forsake thee" (Josh. 1:4–5). In other words, "As you walk in this sphere of influence, everything will bow to My authority in you."

This reveals one of the biggest problems in the church today. Many of us aren't in the place where God has given us authority. We're not operating in our place of divine assignment. We're struggling against divine impulse, like Paul was before Jesus confronted him in the book of Acts. Jesus told him, "I am Jesus whom thou persecutest: *it is* hard for thee to kick against the pricks [*divine impulse¹*]....*Arise,* and go into the city" (Acts 9:5–6, *emphasis mine*).

Paul was like many believers: traveling his own path, sensing what God wanted him to do, and doing his own thing anyway. Paul had a sense of destiny, but in struggling against it, he was actually destroying what God created him to build. Let me exhort you—don't struggle against divine impulse. Give up your will and surrender to God...*because when you begin to walk in the place of your assignment,* nothing will be able to prosper against you all the days of your life!

So arise! Settle it in your mind that no matter what, you're going to follow God's path to abundance. And then whatever people say or do against you won't prosper because you're walking in another realm. Threats and insults can't reach the throne of God. They have to fall back down to where they came from; and one day, they'll be put to ashes.

Once God clarified the boundaries of his authority, He told Joshua, "Be strong and of a good courage: for unto this people shalt thou divide for an inheritance the land, which I sware unto their fathers to give them" (Josh. 1:6). *This reveals a vital prophetic principle:* When God calls you to an assignment that will fulfill a covenant promise, you're going to stand against opposition. It's not going to be easy, because the enemy will do everything in his power to abort it.

If you're an entrepreneur, this means that nobody is going to encourage you but you. So you have to learn how to wake up each day and say, "God has prospered me." It doesn't matter what your checkbook balance says, how your finances looked last year, or what you think they'll look like next year…*you have to speak what you hear in your spirit.* You have to be strong and very courageous, because what you're doing is not only going to affect your pocket book, *it's going to change the economy.* It's going to provide people with jobs to support their families and goods and services to help them possess what God has for them. So you must be strong *and* willing to go it alone, if necessary, to come into your full inheritance.

I can hear God saying to Joshua, "I'm about to set you up. Right now, it looks bleak because everybody's mourning over Moses' death, but *you've* got to be strong—and not just for what's happening now. You've got to be courageous to do what others haven't been commanded to carry out. You have to be bold enough to try things that others didn't try."

Let's say you've started a new restaurant. You'll have to be bold enough to put some new items on the menu that people never thought would work…knowing (because you've already spied out the land) that once they've tasted it, they'll come back to your restaurant again and again…*because you were courageous.* Perhaps you're a printer. Then you need to mix those dyes together in a creative way to come up with a unique color— something way "outside of the box" that grabs people's attention and doesn't copy someone else's product. *You've got to be courageous enough to break the cycle.*

This is why God told Joshua to be courageous three times, to set new life into motion—because God knows the only way

Joshua would possess the Promised Land was to be strong enough to survive the critics. The same applies to you. As soon as you start trying to be different, everybody's going to say, "Oh, you're trying to be grand; you're trying to be *this* or *that.*" *Here's the prophetic principle:* If you know God is with you and where He wants you to go, criticism won't matter...because you've received God's Word that He won't fail you—and that will be enough.

Declaring the Word of the Lord

Let's move on to verses 8 and 9 of Joshua 1:

This book of the law shall not depart out of thy mouth; but thou shalt meditate therein day and night, that thou mayest observe to do according to all that is written therein: for then thou shalt make thy way prosperous, and then thou shalt have good success. Have not I commanded thee? Be strong and of a good courage; be not afraid, neither be thou dismayed: for the Lord thy God is with thee withersoever thou goest.

The first prophetic principle this reveals is that you have the ability to speak the Word of the Lord over yourself. After all, what you say to yourself affects you more than it does anyone else! So if you start speaking doubt or weakness, it will affect you *first.* That's why God told Joshua to meditate on the Word and keep it in his mouth at all times.

I can hear God saying, "Joshua, I'm putting you on the path to wealth. Don't hold back what gives you legal access to it. Keep My Word in your spirit, and every time you come to a cross-roads, you'll start speaking the right thing. Don't get to a place where you need water and can't speak it out of a rock, because the enemy will try to make you change what you say. If he can do this, he'll be able to change your atmosphere by bringing people around you who match your confession of unbelief—only their words will be even worse. They'll criticize you, bring up your past, and remind you of your weaknesses and short-comings. And you don't need that, Joshua. So stay in My Word. Don't go to the left or to the right. Don't deviate. Don't let My Word stop flowing out of your mouth because what you say reflects who you are. You've become a *living soul,* and you can only prosper when the law of creation, Genesis, is operating from within you."

Listen to me. This is why your soul must prosper before any-thing else can. God wants *you* to start creating the right spiritual atmosphere for things to happen. Then *you've* got to be able to expand the vision once it comes into fruition. Then *you've* got to learn how to come into divine order and manage what He's given you so that God can bless it. Then *you've* got to learn to walk in accountability and integrity so that you can identify how the Lord increases you. And then, finally, you have to learn how to expect the overflow.

Joshua had come through this prophetic process, so his mouth had the power to bring *whatsoever* was out of order *into order.* That way when criticism came, his conversation exposed that which was evil. This can happen for you today. As you keep your conversation right, people will begin to know when their words don't line up with the Word of God. And they'll either have to change or shut up and leave you alone because your words have released the creative power of God to change the atmosphere.

Think about when Moses talked to a rock. Some people probably wanted to lock him up and throw away the key. *It sounded crazy!* I can just hear it, "Moses, what are you doing?"

"I'm about to talk to a rock."

"What do you mean, you're about to talk to a rock?"

"I'm about to bring out of a rock something you couldn't find."

This reveals another prophetic principle: *Courageous people find stuff that other people pass over.* The whole time, people were leaning against the rock thinking, "This is a good place to rest, but I just wish I had some water." And it was there all the time! (See Num. 20:8).

Jesus said, "Whosoever drinketh of the water that I shall give him shall never thirst; but the water that I shall give him shall be *in him* a well of water springing up into everlasting life. He that believeth on me, as the scripture hath said, *out of his belly* shall flow rivers of living water" (John 4:14; 7:38, *emphasis mine*). Your belly digests whatever you put in your mouth, so keep eating God's Word and it will *spring up* when you need it.

The Dilemma of the Rock

When I started studying the rock that Moses spoke to in Numbers 20, I was curious whether it had been soaking up the rain that had fallen on it for so many years, or was the rock simply tapped into a well that no one could see? One way or the other, God prepared it. We don't know if the rock was hollow on the inside and was actually soaking up water (that no one knew about), or if it had the ability to tap into resources that were deep under the surface—ready to bring forth water at Moses' voice. To be honest, I think the rock was tapped into water from its Source.

Why? God can cause *rivers of living water* to come out of your belly, so to me this rock prophetically represents our ability to unlock living waters from God's kingdom through Jesus Christ. Jesus was talking about *Peter's confession* when He said, "Thou art Peter, and upon this rock I will build my church; and the gates of hell shall not prevail against it" (Matt. 16:18). So the "keys" to the kingdom of heaven are also in your mouth. "*Whatsoever* thou shalt bind on earth shall be bound in heaven; and *whatsoever* thou shalt loose on earth shall be loosed in heaven" (Matt. 16:19, *emphasis mine*).

Taming your tongue is like drawing water out of a rock; that's why James 3:8 says, "But the tongue can no man tame." Nevertheless, Jesus—*the living Word*—can do it *supernaturally.* If you submit to Him as Lord, He'll use your mouth to unlock the victory in areas you never thought were possible. Jesus is saying to you today, "Speak those things that are 'not as though they were' (Rom. 4:17), because when you speak, *it will come to pass*—because I AM the Rock!"

Your words can become rivers of living water that somebody else can drink. They can bring somebody's spirit back to life. Your words can quicken someone who's suffering from spiritual dehydration and cause them to *see* and *do* the will of God. The gates of hell shall not prevail! *And this is why Joshua had to rise to the challenge.*

I can hear God saying, "Joshua, if you let My Word depart, you're going to have major problems, because hell will be able to take over your legal access to the wealth I've prepared for you." Instead, you'll have legal access to worry, because worry will come out of your soul, "How's it going to happen? When is it going to take place? Are you sure? It doesn't make sense. I've never tried this before."

God said, "But thou shalt meditate therein day and night" (Josh. 1:8). In other words, keep your focus right, because whatever you put in your mouth will determine how you prosper.

Let's say you're booking a flight. "Hello, I want to take a flight. Uh, I want to fly from, uh you know, um…what's that airport up there by Baltimore? Well, you work for the airlines, don't you? Which airline? Oh yeah, it's BWI. Yeah, that's right…I heard of that one before. Exactly, that's it. Well, I want to fly from BWI. Uh, my girlfriend said we could catch a flight out to somewhere near Phoenix. They've got a nice place there, so I just wanted to find just how much this costs. What's the cheapest ticket you have?" If this is you, you need to correct your communication!

First of all, never say *cheapest;* instead, say *least expensive*— because it tells people you don't have money when you say cheap. *Least expensive* says that you're conservative. You respect money and you don't waste it. *Cheap* says you can't afford it, no matter what they tell you, so you're going to have to call back once you know if you have enough money. "Uh, hold on baby, I have to call you back. Is this the number I can reach you at?" And because you need the cheapest price, now you have to talk to Bill, Sam, John, and whomever else to get enough money to pay for the ticket.

This is similar to what God was doing with Joshua. He was developing something in Joshua's spirit that would give him the ability to take his heart to another level. So the correct communication would be, "Good afternoon. How are you? Great! I'd like to investigate the flight and ticket options going from BWI to Phoenix International. Would you be so kind as to give me these rates? And if you happen to notice any special days where the rates are better because of the market, let me know. Also, I'm on my cell phone right now, so could you please write down my number in case we get disconnected? I really appreciate your time." *How you communicate makes a world of difference.*

Joshua learned to line up his communication with what God was speaking. Let's look at it from the perspective of the prophetic code. In his first command, he declared that Israel would cross over the Jordan to possess the land (see Josh. 1:10-11). His second command was to send spies into Jericho (2:1). When the spies returned, his third command was for the people to sanctify themselves [3]. His fourth command was for and the priests to carry the ark of the covenant [4] before the people into the Jordan (see Josh. 3:5–6).

Joshua's fifth command was significant: "And Joshua said unto the children of Israel, Come hither, and hear the words of the Lord your God" (3:9). He had become *strong and very courageous,* because by grace [5], he declared the Word of God. And his sixth command (the number of man), Joshua commanded Israel to cross the Jordan: "And it shall come to pass, as soon as the soles of the feet of the priests that bear the ark of the Lord, the Lord of all the earth, shall rest in the waters of Jordan, that the waters of Jordan shall be cut off from the waters that come down from above; and they shall stand upon an heap" (Josh. 3:13). And it came to pass exactly as Joshua had declared it.

Joshua gave the seventh command after Israel crossed over, which *perfected* their journey: "Then Joshua called the twelve men....take you up every man of you a stone upon his shoulder, according unto the number of the tribes of the children of Israel: That this may be a sign among you, that when your children ask their fathers in time to come..." (Josh. 4:4–6). And his eighth command brought in the new day: "Joshua therefore commanded the priests, saying, Come ye up out of Jordan" (Josh. 4:17).

So what's my point? Joshua had to cross over before he could lead Israel across the Jordan into the Promised Land. He crossed over from despair into the joy of the Lord. He crossed over from doubt into absolute faith. He crossed over from timidity into being strong and courageous...*and a nation was birthed into a new day.* Joshua 4:14 says, "On that day the Lord magnified Joshua in the sight of all Israel; and they feared him, as they feared Moses, all the days of his life."

You can walk in the divine authority God intended for His children from the beginning—just cross over into a new day.

Cross over into your destiny. Will you be obedient to continue following God's path and cross over into corporate wealth and accountability? If so, Isaiah 1:19 has promised, "If ye be willing and obedient, ye shall eat the good of the land."

So far, you've learned how to prosper in your own soul...*now* God can use you to help build a nation. And as you declare His Word, you'll make your way prosperous. You'll unlock *living waters* deep inside your soul and enjoy good success. Tell me, are you ready to multiply what He's given you and enter the joy of your Lord? Then it's time to move to a new dimension of blessing and accountability—*where your words will give life to many.* Yes, you can be rich—or you can cross over into true wealth and abundance through Jesus Christ. Which will you choose?

7

~~~~

AND THOU SHALT MAKE
THY WAY PROSPEROUS

*Get wisdom, get understanding: forget it not; neither decline
from the words of my mouth.*

*Forsake her not, and she shall preserve thee: love her, and she
shall keep thee (Prov. 4:5-6).*

When Israel crossed over the Jordan, it not only
marked a change in leadership, but also a change in
divine strategy. God wanted Israel to multiply but in a different
way. He had overshadowed them and prospered their souls; now
He was commanding them to take dominion and increase their
wealth. God said to Joshua, "Be strong and of a good courage:
for unto this people shalt thou divide for an inheritance the
land, which I sware unto their fathers to give them" (Josh. 1:6).

In other words, "Be strong and courageous, because you're
going to actively pursue what I've already told you to do—
which will ultimately give you *the ability* to divide the land for
an inheritance." This reveals an important prophetic principle:
It's vital for believers to come into ownership, to actually possess

more land. You can always lease an apartment, but you have to abide by the owner's rules and guidelines to remain on the property. When you become an owner, you set the rules because you have a legal right to do it. So it was vital for Israel to repossess the land of their inheritance—because unless they took possession, they couldn't fulfill the corporate covenant.

Stay with me, I'm going somewhere here. In the beginning, God created everything Adam would ever need and then put him in the Garden to maintain it (Gen. 2:8,15). He gave Adam dominion over *every living thing that moved upon the earth* (Gen. 1:28). I believe one of the reasons is that he never had to pay the price to take the Garden in the first place. He didn't understand what it meant to take the land. Later, with Israel, God took them into the Promised Land, but He required them to play an active role in obtaining their inheritance—thus transitioning them, through experience, into ownership.

The prophetic principle here is this: You value what you invest in. That's part of being an owner. You take better care of the things that you've worked hard to acquire. You guard and manage them carefully. And that includes looking out for the interests of others. Corporate accountability protects the interests of the nation. Oh yes, it was definitely a new day.

The Call to Active Duty

For Israel, the new season of destiny was a call to constant warfare. They had faced enemies before crossing over, but now it was going to a new level. And Joshua began to receive strategies for waging war. Israel was about to become a nation of divine warriors because when they crossed over, the shadow of the Lord lifted—and their enemies could see they were coming (Josh. 5:1; 6:1). They actually started to track Israel's exploits, so Joshua needed to call upon God daily for wisdom to be effective, victorious—strategic—in battle.

Many believers today are shocked when they discover their call to faith is a call to warfare. Jesus said, "Think not that I am come to send peace on earth: I came not to send peace, but a sword. He that loveth father or mother more than me is not worthy of me: and he that loveth son or daughter more than me is not worthy of me. And he that taketh not his cross, and followeth after me, is not worthy of me. He that findeth his life shall lose it: and he that loseth his life for my sake shall find it" (Matt. 10:34,37–39).

Whether you realize it or not, when you get saved you've entered the realm of warfare because you're under a corporate anointing. You are related to Christ, but you also have a place of corporate responsibility. You are God's child, which means Jesus has something for you to accomplish—and you'll soon discover it's part of the bigger picture. You have become an active part of the wealth of the nation. You are interdependent. You have become one with other believers—because certain battles require pulling all of our resources *together.*

A Time for Action

Let's go back to Joshua 1:8–9:

This book of the law shall not depart out of thy mouth; but thou shalt meditate therein day and night, that thou mayest observe to do according to all that is written therein: for then thou shalt make thy way prosperous, and then thou shalt have good success. Have not I commanded thee? Be strong and of a good courage; be not afraid, neither be thou dismayed: for the Lord thy God is with thee whithersoever thou goest.

It's clear. Meditating on the Word and confessing the Word are supposed to lead to action. Action leads to prosperity, and prosperity opens the door to good success. And God will be with you *as you go.* So after you let go of the past, you have to move into the future...and that's exactly what Israel had begun to do. Joshua 4:13 says, "About forty thousand prepared for war passed over before the Lord unto battle, to the plains of Jericho." They were ready for battle even before the priests came out of the river!

You have entered a season of divine strategy and wealth, which means (to take from a popular saying), you'll begin to let God grant you either the serenity to accept what you can't change or the courage to change what you can; and, most importantly, the wisdom to know the difference. *So here's the prophetic principle:* To possess our inheritance, we must learn how to receive the strategy of the Lord—whatever it may be—and act on it.

Let's say you're exploring a new job opportunity. Be strategic and dress in season. Don't walk in looking like you got saved before you were born—wearing a black suit and a huge, glowing Jesus pin. You'll look like you just came from a funeral! Never wear black on an interview. Instead, wear brown, charcoal gray, or navy blue. And if you don't have one of these colors, wear burgundy. If you're daring, you could wear a light forest green, but strategically, in the right season.

Wisdom would tell you to wear green in the spring, because that's when people are looking for something that reminds them new life is about to come. If you don't understand the value of strategy, you'll go into new opportunities dead black. People need to see life, color, and vibrancy.

A Divine Pause

Let's go back to Joshua and the next step in God's strategy. Israel was ready to fight, but God stopped them—because it was time to set some things in order, "But all the people that were born in the wilderness by the way as they came forth out of Egypt, them they had not circumcised" (Josh. 5:5). Moses didn't forget to circumcise them; it was God's prophetic strategy. God wanted to wait and cut a new covenant with a new generation for a new level of soul prosperity. After Joshua obeyed the Lord, He told him, "This day have I rolled away the reproach of Egypt from off you" (Josh. 5:9).

Soon after, the manna (supernatural food from heaven) stopped, "Neither had the children of Israel manna any more; but they did eat of the fruit of the land of Canaan that year" (Josh. 5:12). *This reveals another prophetic principle:* A new strategy requires new provision. By eating the food of the land, Israel would be equipped to possess it.

Many times we don't understand why God brings some things to an end and keeps other things going. This is when you need to remember: You've been born into a new nation, so God's going to start leading you by divine strategy. You have to learn how to stay close to Him to keep in step when He starts moving in a new direction. When He turns, you turn. When He pauses, you pause. And when He moves forward, you possess what He's put in front of you.

If you're going to complete the process of Joshua 1:8 and "make thy way prosperous," you have to deal with things that can tie you to the past; things He's given you the ability to change. This means you have to deal with bad habits. Realistically, you won't be able to change every one before you go to war; but God will put you on pause every now and then to identify and deal with specific areas to keep you from losing ground.

I've got a very bad habit. I don't sleep a lot, so when I'm tired, I really snore...loudly. My wife has told me she has to go into another room until the snoring stops. That gave me a choice. I could either pace myself so that I don't snore her out of the bedroom during the first four hours, or keep doing things the same way and ignore it. The fact is, I know my threshold. I know how much sleep I should be getting. I know when I'm tired, and when I've gone over the limit.

So I had to be honest with myself. I needed to change...and though it wouldn't be easy, I knew it would improve our quality of life. That's when I said, "I'm going to change some things. I'm going to stop taking early morning flights, even though I love them. I'm going to take later flights so that I can get more rest. I'm going to break late working patterns and get to bed at a decent hour."

For you, it could be keeping your gas tank filled. You know that if it falls below a quarter of a tank, you could get stuck in traffic and end up stranded; yet you still go to the station and say, "Five dollars on pump number three." Do you actually want to experience the same thing tomorrow (because anybody can burn five dollars of gas in a day)? Break the habit! Fill up the tank, put in twenty dollars' worth—and know what it feels like to drive freely for three to four days.

Bad habits can stop us from prospering because they break our rhythm. They interrupt our consistency and continuity. They distract our focus. But once you come into focus, things will begin to move because focus advances your faith to another level. You can then enter the realm of receiving true divine strategy. You'll know exactly what to ask of God, and you'll be able to hear Him more clearly. To God, that makes the pause worthwhile.

There are times when you think *circumstances* have forced you into a certain place; but what's *really* happening is that God's pausing to adjust you before allowing you to move forward. That way the enemy won't find any holes in your armor. By forcing you to deal with bad habits, He's actually causing you to move into realms of the Spirit you didn't think you were ready for. And He's saying, "I'm going to get you to the place where I can bless you. If I can just get you there, I'll bless you more than you can imagine."

The Jericho Strategy

Now let's move to Joshua 6:1–2. "Now Jericho was straitly shut up because of the children of Israel: none went out, and none came in. And the Lord said unto Joshua, See, I have given into thine hand Jericho, and the king thereof, and the mighty men of valour." This reveals two things: First of all, Joshua didn't receive the strategy for Jericho until he got there. And second, every entry was *shut, blocked, closed*…and the Lord said this was good news!

Too often, when God puts a pause in our progress (to deal with us personally), we stop altogether. Joshua didn't stop; he paused, and then got up and kept moving toward the goal. You have to remember that you've been commissioned to do a covenant work. So when God pauses you to bring clarity in a certain area, you need to pick up and start moving forward again when He's done—because now you're operating on covenant level. The fate of nations rests in your hands. You've been commissioned to take His Word from Jerusalem, into all Judea, Samaria, and the uttermost parts of the earth (see Acts 1:8).

Another common mistake is we tend to think closed doors mean *God's not in it*. Wrong. According to God's strategy for Jericho, the city was closed up *because* it was *ripe for the taking*. So God continued to shift His strategy and change His methods, to keep Joshua seeking Him for wisdom. He opened the Jordan and then closed up Jericho—*and both meant the same thing*. Move forward. Possess.

It's like the Lord was saying to Joshua, "My son, if thou wilt receive my words, and hide my commandments with thee; so that thou incline thine ear unto wisdom, and apply thine heart to understanding; then shalt thou understand the fear of the Lord, and find the knowledge of God. He layeth up sound wisdom for the righteous: he is a buckler to them that walk uprightly" (Prov. 2:1-2,5,7). In other words, "Joshua, I've prospered your soul.

Now you have to keep prospering it to hear and follow My strategy. And as you apply My wisdom, it will shield you in the time of war."

Now this is interesting. After receiving God's strategy to conquer Jericho—marching around the city one time for six days, then seven times on the seventh day; and each of these days seven priests would march in front holding seven trumpets; then at the sound of the trumpet on the seventh day, all the people would shout and the city wall would collapse and the people would spoil the city—*Joshua issued a new command.* "Ye shall not shout, nor make any noise with your voice, neither shall any word proceed out of your mouth, until the day I bid you shout; then shall ye shout" (Josh. 6:10).

Up to this point Israel had moved from place to place, but they hadn't applied strategy to possess a specific location. To do this, they had to silence individual expression. Now listen to me because this is important. Each person had to learn to blend his or her voice with others: saying the *same thing,* at the *same time,* with the *same depth and intensity.*

If one person had disobeyed, Israel would have been defeated. Why? God was bringing them into corporate responsibility in order to reestablish the nation. He was harmonizing their spirits to obtain wealth. Like I said before, when you want to move out of the individual status of being rich—the next step is to network, blend with others to achieve a collective goal—and that's when results are multiplied.

Wealth Building Strategies

One of the major dilemmas we face in building wealth is many of us have bad or no credit, weak vision, or a slave mentality that's satisfied with always picking up the leftovers. Let me explain. You are a child of God, not a slave. A Canaanite woman once came to Jesus begging for her demon-possessed daughter to be healed, and He replied, "I am not sent but unto the lost sheep of the house of Israel. It is not meet to take the children's bread, and to cast it to dogs" (Matt. 15:24,26).

There are untold riches in Christ Jesus. Are you sure that you know Him? Then there's something you need to know: "For all the promises of God in him are yea, and in him Amen, unto the glory of God by us" (2 Cor. 1:20). In other words, every promise is already done as you remain in Christ to the glory of God. *Even as your soul prospers,* you don't have to settle for crumbs!

Never be satisfied with doing as little as you can. Don't just do one thing well and then be content to be average at everything else. Diversify your portfolio; build additional skills—take two years and develop abilities in another area. Multiply! Otherwise, you'll get stuck in the rut of always doing the same thing day in and day out. If you stay in this mode, you'll get stuck working at fast food restaurants, frying burgers and French fries...*making bricks all day long.* Learn how to become an accountant, or a business manager; maybe you'd like to become a teacher or a self-sufficient entrepreneur. Don't just fall into place waiting for somebody else to get fired so that you can get hired. Create your own opportunity while contributing to the well-being of others. Step up to corporate wealth and abundance.

Use your God-given ability to create...start a day care business in a vacant building. *Think ownership,* "If I start a day care here, I know there's a couple of million dollars I can secure in the next two years to make it happen." *Be bold!* Be courageous. Apply for an loan through the Small Business Administration and get more than enough to start your business. Then the families in your community can be blessed by the excellent services you provide. You're contributing to the wealth of a nation.

Great people create vision because God is a visionary. No one can create like Him. He's been coming up with creative strategies since the beginning of time—*why not listen to Him?* I can't walk by a building that's closed and boarded up without feeling something creative rising up in me. I can always find something to fill a void, if I have the time to do it. It's that creative unction of God. And if you hearken unto His voice when He wants to create something new through you, it will turn your world into a new and better place.

When God told Joshua, "Be strong and of a good courage: for unto this people shalt thou divide for an inheritance the land, which I sware unto their fathers to give them" (Josh. 1:6), He was saying, "I'm giving you my solemn oath, because I don't lie. You will be able to divide this land because it will fulfill My Word to your forefathers. I sware on My ability to be consistent that you'll conquer every obstacle and possess the land. Only you must be willing to go beyond your comfort zone."

Are you broke? Then get a broom and find a store with a lot of leaves and trash in the parking lot. Before anybody shows up for business, clean it up, sweep all the debris way to the back, and don't charge anything. Repeat this for five days and let the management see and appreciate how clean it is. Greet them when they arrive and then walk away. They'll come looking for you. Create an opportunity for yourself! Tell them, "I'll keep this place immaculate...How much will it cost? I tell you what, if you pay me this amount per hour or per week, I'll paint, clean, and even serve as your parking attendant all day long." You've crossed over into corporate anointing—you're going beyond your boundaries—taking ownership of *little* so that God can entrust you with *much.*

Creative people learn how to do something. And by doing so, they solve somebody else's problem...and people that solve problems get promoted. Oh yes, you can do this! All you need is the strategy of the Lord. Ask Him...He's filled with creative ideas—or don't you think God can help you to be more industrious? One day, two blind men followed Jesus, "crying, and saying, Thou Son of David, have mercy on us....and Jesus saith unto them, Believe ye that I am able to do this? They said unto him, Yea, Lord. Then touched he their eyes, saying, According to your faith be it unto you" (Matt. 9:27–29).

Think about it. How could two blind men follow Jesus into a house? They pressed beyond their comfort zone. They leaned on rocks, grabbed onto other people, fell into trees, and maybe even crawled on the ground to create their opportunity. I can just hear Jesus asking, "Do you believe that I can give you new vision? Then you can have it because you created the atmosphere for Me to do it." Create your own atmosphere. Break out of the box. Create an opportunity to prosper.

Let's say you go to work and notice that everybody's papers are out of order, so you spend twenty extra minutes making sure everything's right. "Well, Jim, I just wanted to make sure all the files for this company were in order; I put them over there. Now this company's file is over here, because I remember the last time you were looking for the folder, you couldn't find it—so here are all the company files. I put each category in a different color and cross-referenced them, so when you're working on the green category, you know exactly which companies to pull. Now the orange represents this category...blue...yellow," and so on.

You just solved Jim's problem. You just got promoted because you were courageous enough to take initiative and organize the information that other people just stacked to the side, causing Jim to wait forty minutes to find a piece of paper. So from now on when he brings in a new company, he's going to send it to you so that you can put it in the right order. You see, you've moved up to corporate anointing. And as you benefit the company, you'll prosper as well.

Start solving problems and get promoted. Possess the land! Don't wait for somebody to approach you and say, "I have a problem...find a way to solve it." Tap your creative potential in God! Follow divine strategy and create your own opportunity. March around that city, blow the trumpet, and give a victory shout! That wall's coming down.

A New Direction for the Future

I hear the voice of the Spirit declaring new things, in three major areas, that can revolutionize the church as we know it.

First, by applying sound business strategies under the direction of the Holy Spirit, many believers will learn how to become debt free. You could enter into a new realm: your house could become your office; and your business could become so profitable, it could pay your mortgage, and so on. God's going to pour out an entrepreneurial anointing and specific wisdom for His people to have good success.

Second, He's going to move us into ownership of property—to the extent that we can divide it with others. There are vacant properties everywhere, and God's going to give special wisdom and ability to secure them. You may be presented with an opportunity to own a property that's too small for you—buy it anyway! Make it work. If you need five bedrooms and it only has two, then rent the property to someone else and let it generate revenue for you. Wisdom.

Third, take the limits off. Stop limiting God. Make a decision to lose your measuring stick, because with what God's getting ready to do, it's going to be too short anyway. When you hear the strategy of the Lord for your situation, don't stop short because you don't understand exactly how everything's going to play out. God may require you to go all the way to Jericho before He reveals the complete strategy. He may lead you to the edge of the river before it opens a path for you to cross over. Wisdom.

Take ownership of every opportunity God presents to you. Possess the land, and bring others with you. Then you'll have every right to guard and manage your inheritance under God's direction.

8

~~~~~~

LEGAL ACCESS TO WEALTH

But thou shalt remember the Lord thy God: for it is he that giveth thee power to get wealth, that he may establish his covenant which he sware unto thy fathers, as it is this day (Deut. 8:18).

It was definitely a new day. Israel had come into their divine destiny and the nation had been reborn. They were conquering kingdoms and walking in corporate wealth and abundance—*because they'd obeyed the voice of the Lord.* Israel had gained legal access to the wealth of the nations by following a *written* Law (that God had established) *by faith.* Let me explain.

In Genesis 17, God made a covenant with Abraham when he was ninety-nine years old. Prophetically, two *nines* not only represented divine agreement, but also a double birthing (hence, being reborn or born again). God declared to Abraham, "I am the Almighty God; walk before me, and be thou perfect. And I will make my covenant between me and thee, and will multiply thee exceedingly" (Gen. 17:1–2). In the verses that followed, He promised Abraham the land of Canaan as an inheritance (see vs. 4–8).

155

~~~~~~

Yet it was conditional—every "man child" had to be circumcised when he was eight days old (see vs. 9–12). So the act of circumcision would birth a new day (representing number 8). This spoke in the prophetic on two levels because Abraham was ninety-nine years old. First, Israel would be reborn (the first nine) before they took Jericho and possessed the land of Canaan as God promised. Then, Christ would give the eternal kingdom to all who were born again by receiving Him (the second 9).

Why is circumcision significant? Genesis 17:13 says, "And my covenant shall be in your flesh for an everlasting covenant." So God gave His Word in their flesh to equip them to prosper. Later, Jesus came in human flesh and completed the prophetic process. And all who trusted in Him would live an abundant life.

This also demonstrated another prophetic principle: You must decrease before you increase in the kingdom of God. In other words, God humbles you in order to prepare you for true greatness. He makes sure that you magnify Him when you have *little* and when you have *much*. In a spiritual sense, He *cuts* your "flesh" to help you be spiritually productive. That's definitely been my experience. Jesus said, "Every branch in me that beareth not fruit he taketh away: and every branch that beareth fruit, he purgeth it, that it may bring forth more fruit" (John 15:2).

Remember, Abraham didn't receive *exceeding multiplication* until there was a *cutting*. So when God paused Israel en route to Jericho, He "cut" a new circumcision with a new generation to fulfill the promise. Israel could now obey His Law by faith— the faith of Abraham—which had been revealed through the Law of Moses. God decreased Israel so they could possess what

He'd promised in Abraham's covenant. The final test would be—*how would they handle their victories when the season of warfare subsided?*

The Tablets of the Law Restored

Let's look back again to answer this question. Before dying on mount Nebo, Moses gave the laws of Israel a second time in the book of Deuteronomy.

> *And the Lord said unto Moses, Behold, thy days approach that thou must die: call Joshua, and present yourselves in the tabernacle of the congregation, that I may give him a charge. And Moses and Joshua went, and presented themselves in the tabernacle of the congregation.*
>
> *And the Lord appeared in the tabernacle in a pillar of a cloud: and the pillar of the cloud stood over the door of the tabernacle.*
>
> *And he gave Joshua the son of Nun a charge, and said, Be strong and of a good courage: for thou shalt bring the children of Israel into the land which I sware unto them: and I will be with thee.*
>
> *And it came to pass, when Moses had made an end of writing the words of this law in a book, until they were finished,*
>
> *That Moses commanded the Levites, which bare the ark of the covenant of the Lord, saying,*
>
> *Take this book of the law, and put it in the side of the ark of the covenant of the Lord your God, that it may be there for a witness against thee* (Deut. 31:14–15,23–26).

When God spoke to Joshua after Moses died, He repeated the command to be *strong and courageous* three more times— and the *fourth* time these words were spoken, a supernatural impartation was released (see Josh. 1:6–9). This supernatural strength and courage gave Joshua the ability to uphold the Law. This was *his* legal access to wealth. "Not by might, nor by power, but by my spirit, saith the Lord of hosts" (Zech. 4:6).

Our laws are set up in such a way that anyone who aspires to gain wealth has a legal way to do it. It's illegal to buy a gun, stroll into a bank, and say, "Okay, give me all the money in the drawer…and thanks, *have a nice day.*" It's illegal to sell drugs that destroy people's lives. It's illegal to steal a successful business secret and then market it as your own. The law doesn't cover criminal behavior. So in the spirit realm, if your soul doesn't prosper and give birth to true abundance, you don't have legal access to it. In other words, you're a thief.

Under God's Law, everything would prosper because it followed the pattern of soul prosperity. So if you worship Him, obey His commands, and work honestly, diligently, and faithfully—*you will prosper.*

God reminded Joshua, "Listen, I want you to do everything according to the Law I gave through Moses, whom you served." In other words, "Joshua, you already have this within you. You've walked it out. This is nothing new. You can do it. And as you set the example, others will be able to follow—and you'll possess your inheritance together by trusting in Me."

The Challenge of Mentorship

Many people today suffer from a lack of mentorship. And few are willing to invest the time to *sharpen* others, so they'll find the biblical path to true prosperity. We must value the people God has entrusted to our care and oversight. Moses walked with God and commanded Joshua. Joshua recognized Moses' leadership because he could *see* Moses' walk was *real*. Joshua knew Moses was accountable to God. So Moses could boldly say, "Joshua, you're going to be my minister because you've faithfully stayed up front *with me.*"

This reveals a prophetic principle: People who are called to lead have to step up and be leaders! Moses couldn't sit around, doing what he wanted to do...*undisciplined,* and then expect to raise up a Joshua, who would one day lead a nation to possess their inheritance. Jesus spoke this parable.

> *Who then is that faithful and wise steward, whom his lord shall make ruler over his household, to give them their portion of meat in due season?*
>
> *Blessed is that servant, whom his lord when he cometh shall find so doing.*
>
> *But and if that servant say in his heart, My lord delayeth his coming; and shall begin to beat the menservants and maidens, and to eat and drink, and to be drunken;*
>
> *The lord of that servant will come in a day when he looketh not for him, and at an hour when he is not aware, and will cut him in sunder, and will appoint him his portion with the unbelievers.*
>
> *And that servant, which knew his lord's will, and prepared not himself, neither did according to his will, shall be beaten with many stripes* (Luke 12:42–43,45–47).

As a leader, reading this keeps me accountable—because I realize that when I neglect my duty to mentor others, it can be equated to spiritual abuse. Mentorship is a vital part of the corporate anointing; so much so that Jesus assigned a harsh penalty for those who take it for granted. Please hear me on this: The church cannot be trusted with material wealth until we learn to value *true riches.*

I thank God that my parents mentored me from a young age. By the time I was five years old, I was washing the church van by myself. That was my early wealth training, because my parents knew I had to be *shaped* to develop a leadership spirit. And this is also why God commanded Israel to diligently teach their children the same laws they were to follow (see Deut. 6:6-7). Early wealth training builds corporate anointing and establishes the groundwork for wealth—because *these* children followed Joshua into the Promised Land. These children became warriors.

Mentorship releases generational destiny. God told Joshua, "Only be thou strong and very courageous, that thou mayest observe to do according to all the law, which Moses my servant commanded thee: turn not from it to the right hand or to the left, that thou mayest prosper whithersoever thou goest" (Josh. 1:7). Generational prosperity—corporate anointing—*is unlimited.*

A good mentor will make sure you develop skills to identify many options because the mentor *sharpens* you in many different areas and teaches you to "do according to all the law." A mentor is thorough. Let's say you're going to be a cook. A mentor will teach you how to prepare Chinese, Greek, Italian, Asian, and American entrees (and more). This, in turn, develops your understanding of tastes so that you'll be able to season different foods correctly and add the right amounts to each recipe. And a mentor doesn't stop there: They'll challenge you to learn all about cooking utensils and everything that pertains to being an excellent cook.

A true mentor always challenges you to learn all there is to know about your area of focus—and then encourages you to learn other things. And they won't hesitate to tell you, "You're great at this but limited in this area. You need to learn how to do this." Then they keep reinforcing it until you've mastered it. Mentorship takes time and discipline—and that's why so few truly embrace it.

Jesus said, "Ye know that the princes of the Gentiles exercise dominion over them, and they that are great exercise authority upon them. But it shall not be so among you: but whosoever will be great among you, let him be your minister; And whosoever will be chief among you, let him be your servant: Even as the Son of man came not to be ministered unto, but to minister, and to give his life a ransom for many" (Matt. 20:25–28).

Mentorship follows the pattern of Jesus, so it releases a corporate anointing that never stops flowing. *Yes, it's truly unlimited because it's eternal.* So if God is calling you to mentor others, let Philippians 2:5–11 challenge you.

Let this mind be in you, which was also in Christ Jesus:

Who, being in the form of God, thought it not robbery to be equal with God:

But made himself of no reputation, and took upon him the form of a servant, and was made in the likeness of men:

And being found in fashion as a man, he humbled himself, and became obedient unto death, even the death of the cross.

Wherefore God also hath highly exalted him, and given him a name which is above every name:

That at the name of Jesus every knee should bow, of things in heaven and things in earth, and things under the earth;

And that every tongue should confess that Jesus Christ is Lord, to the glory of God the Father.

The Call to Greatness

God was calling Joshua to greatness. He was challenging him to lead a nation to a place they'd never known. "Listen, Joshua, I want you to go over the Jordan, where nobody else has ever stood, and then reclaim it for your inheritance. And always remember this land, so you can lead My people to it." When God calls you to greatness, He'll challenge you to redefine what others think is impossible. So get ready. God's going to tap your potential. And He'll challenge you to follow through, even while others are calling you crazy.

Stop being weak and timid. *Start being strong and very courageous.* Learn to start celebrating your next level of discipline: Don't ever get so comfortable that you just lay back and let the chips fall where they may. You've been designed to prosper *even as your soul prospers,* so what's already living *inside of you* will prosper *outside of you.* You have to develop the ability to go within yourself and see yourself owning, operating, possessing, utilizing, embracing, and experiencing *whatsoever* God has revealed to your heart. For example, if you can't see yourself owning a Kentucky Fried Chicken and receiving royalty checks, then please don't expect it to happen. The call to greatness.

God is empowering us by challenging us, so that we'll arise and maximize our potential. He's equipping us to conquer by causing us to actively possess our inheritance. He's building the wealth of His people. And this means African Americans, Caucasians, Hispanics, Asians, and Indians—every tribe and nation that confesses Jesus Christ is Lord. God is calling us to arise and diversify, so that we'll become rich in God and bless His creation with the wealth He's already provided.

Start networking with somebody else and become wealthy! Obey God and let Him bless you to the point where you can approach someone and say, "I want to invest $40,000 in your company and all I want is a 2 percent return, because God told me He's going to challenge you to make four million dollars. I know my $40,000 investment's going to yield a quick return over the next two years. And I want an option to buy four more years when the first two are up." Diversification is multiplication—and that's the difference between becoming rich and obtaining wealth. You can't become wealthy by yourself. You could inherit money and become rich, but you can't generate wealth without working strategically with others.

The Decision to Prosper Is Yours

God has placed a world of opportunity at our fingertips, but we must choose to follow the right path. *Soul dominion and prosperity are conditional.* Yes, God does give us the power to gain wealth, but it comes with a warning: "Beware that thou forget not the Lord thy God, in not keeping his commandments, and his judgments, and his statutes, which I command thee this day: Lest when thou hast eaten and art full, and hast built goodly houses, and dwelt therein; and when thy herds and thy flocks multiply, and thy silver and thy gold is multiplied, and all that thou hast is multiplied; Then thine heart be lifted up, and thou forget the Lord thy God..." (Deut. 8:11–14).

Have you ever hit a big pothole and your front alignment starts going off? That's when you start noticing all of the little ones—but they didn't cause the problem! Yet we blame the little potholes for the damage. This happens spiritually. We drive into potholes by refusing to obey everything God commands us to do. Then we wonder why we're headed in the wrong direction. We wonder why it slowly becomes more difficult to respond to His voice. *Here's a warning:* You can't keep hitting every pothole, because eventually...*something's going to give.*

"Well, I'm not going to church tonight...I don't feel like praying...I'll read the Bible tomorrow...." Potholes. "Oh no, here comes another offering plate...I gave last week, I'm not giving tonight." Potholes. And then you wonder why you keep running off the road! Your wheels are wobbly; they're turning out of control. "Now I know this is the devil trying to run me off the highway." Not so. You hit a pothole; you got lazy and then started hitting everything you should have avoided. You started running over stuff that wasn't even between the lines! And then you blamed it on the devil. No, you have to make the right choices—choose the path that leads to biblical abundance.

Deuteronomy 11:26–28 says, "Behold, I set before you this day a blessing and a curse; A blessing, if you obey the commandments of the Lord your God:... And a curse, if ye will not obey the commandments of the Lord your God, but turn aside out of the way which I command you this day, to go after other gods, which ye have not known." You have a choice...and remember, whatever you allow to *master you* becomes your god. And the sad thing is; you often don't recognize it until it slaps you in the face.

Now let's go back to Genesis. Adam and Eve were born into wealth...*and it was good.* They were challenged to take dominion...*and that was good.* Then something unexpected happened: "And the Lord God commanded the man, saying, Of every tree of the garden thou mayest freely eat: But of the tree of the knowledge of good and evil, thou shalt not eat of it: for in the day that thou eatest thereof thou shalt surely die" (Gen. 2:16–17).

As soon as God commanded Adam *not* to do something, the problem started. First of all, why did the serpent come to the woman? Could it be that Eve was his only option? God had commanded Adam, so the serpent didn't have authority to approach him. And even if he wasn't standing with Eve when the temptation began—*Adam was perfect*—he had the ability to discern that something was going on.

So Adam watched the scene unfold and did nothing. "After all," he could have thought, "God didn't say *she* couldn't eat the fruit." Maybe Adam thought he was exercising his dominion authority by letting the whole thing play out. And when Eve didn't shrivel up and die right on the spot, he took the fruit and ate it...because deep down, he'd desired that fruit from the beginning and couldn't have it. Maybe Adam was looking for a loophole—or should I say a pothole?

What Adam didn't realize was, by withholding his authority, *he allowed the serpent to master him.* The devil snared Adam with the same deception that had gotten him cast out of the mountain of God (see Ezek. 28:12–19). So the serpent robbed man's inheritance and became the god of this world (see 2 Cor. 4:2–4). Maybe this is why Paul said, "But have renounced the hidden things of dishonesty, not walking in craftiness, nor handling the word of God deceitfully; but by manifestation of the truth commending ourselves to every man's conscience in the sight of God" (2 Cor. 4:2).

Adam and Eve didn't stay on the path of eternal abundance, so they lost their prosperity. They broke the pattern: They *walked* in the counsel of the ungodly, *stood* in the way of sinners, and *sat* in the seat of the scornful...so they were driven away, "like the chaff" (Ps. 1:4) from the land of their divine inheritance. And it passed down to the next generation.

We've already talked about Cain and Abel, but let's look at another angle. Cain, the first fruits of their union, was a *tiller of the ground*—and he was living out the curse. That's why he brought an unacceptable offering unto God. He didn't seek after God to know what pleased Him. He walked in the vanity of his own mind. And even after God spoke directly to Cain in Genesis 4:6–7, he ignored the counsel of God and killed his brother Abel (see Gen. 4:8).

Abel, on the other hand, was the second son—the seed of divine agreement. Abel was a keeper of sheep (see Gen. 4:2) and walked in blessings. He, no doubt, had learned to seek after God to know what was pleasing to Him—so he brought an acceptable offering by giving God his best (see Gen. 4:4). Hebrews 11:4 says, "By faith Abel offered unto God a more excellent sacrifice than Cain, by which he obtained witness that he was righteous, God testifying of his gifts: and by it he being dead yet speaketh."

Abel's voice still echoes today, bearing fruit generations after his noble act. Abel knew the meaning of true, biblical prosperity because he prospered in his soul. Cain's story teaches another lesson, which Jesus shared in Luke 12:15–21.

> And he said unto them, Take heed, and beware of covetousness: for a man's life consisteth not in the abundance of the things which he possesseth.
>
> And he spake a parable unto them, saying, The ground of a certain rich man brought forth plentifully:
>
> And he thought within himself, saying, What shall I do, because I have no room where to bestow my fruits?
>
> And he said, This will I do: I will pull down my barns, and build greater; and there will I bestow all my fruits and my goods.
>
> And I will say to my soul, Soul, thou hast much goods laid up for many years; take thine ease, eat, drink, and be merry.
>
> But God said unto him, Thou fool, this night thy soul shall be required of thee: then whose shall those things be, which thou hast provided?
>
> So is he that layeth up treasure for himself, and is not rich toward God.

Let me put it all together. Adam became a *living soul* before God gave him dominion. Therefore, soul prosperity isn't based on what you have. It's based on who you are and how you relate to your heavenly Father. *Are you rich toward God?* Then you're in the place where God can bless you. If not, it's time to examine your soul—because when God brings you into true abundance, He expects you to divide it with others. He wants you to arise, embrace the corporate anointing, and share His wealth—so that His covenant through Jesus Christ will come to completion.

God is setting before you a blessing and a curse, and just like Israel—you have the right to choose which path you will follow.

What Will You Do With Your Inheritance?

Let's go back to Deuteronomy 31:16-17, when Moses and Joshua went before the Lord in the Tabernacle. God appeared and said to Moses, "Behold, thou shalt sleep with thy fathers; and this people will rise up, and go a whoring after the gods of the strangers of the land, whither they go to be among them, and will forsake me, and break my covenant which I have made with them. Then my anger shall be kindled against them in that day, and I will forsake them, and I will hide my face from them, and they shall be devoured, and many evils and troubles shall befall them; so that they will say in that day, Are not these evils come upon us, because our God is not among us?"

Before his death Joshua challenged Israel: "Now therefore fear the Lord, and serve him in sincerity and in truth: and put away the gods which your fathers served on the other side of the flood, and in Egypt; and serve ye the Lord. And if it seem evil unto you to serve the Lord, choose you this day whom ye will serve" (Josh. 24:14–15). That generation of Israelites chose to serve the Lord. They continued to magnify God even after achieving great wealth in the Promised Land (see Josh 24:31)— because they'd been *cut* in a *new circumcision*. This "born-again" nation had kingdom vision, and they handled their wealth according to God's covenant laws.

Ultimately, the nation lost sight of God's kingdom and fulfilled Moses' prophecy in Deuteronomy 31. Despite excellent leadership and mentorship, Israel began to worship other gods...and the nation's prosperity hung in the balance. Some, though, still knew by faith that the eternal kingdom was coming. "And these all, having obtained a good report through faith, received not the promise: God having provided some better thing for us, that they without us should not be made perfect" (Heb. 11:39–40). Through soul prosperity, they received a deposit on an eternal inheritance.

Let me encourage you today. Even if you've made costly mistakes, God can lead you back to true abundance. He didn't give up on Israel, His chosen people, so the Lord won't give up on you—*but He will challenge you to prosper your soul*. After all, it's the Law. Let me close with this story from Mark 12:28–34.

And one of the scribes came, and having heard them reasoning together, and perceiving that he had answered them well, asked him, Which is the first commandment of all?

And Jesus answered him, The first of all the commandments is, Hear, O Israel; The Lord our God is one Lord:

And thou shalt love the Lord thy God with all thy heart, and with all thy soul, and with all thy mind, and with all thy strength: this is the first commandment.

And the second is like, namely this, Thou shalt love thy neighbour as thyself. There is none other commandment greater than these.

And the scribe said unto him, Well, Master, thou hast said the truth: for there is one God; and there is none other but he:

And to love him with all the heart, and with all the understanding, and with all the soul, and with all the strength, and to love his neighbour as himself, is more than all whole burnt offerings and sacrifices.

And when Jesus saw that he answered discreetly, he said unto him, Thou art not far from the kingdom of God....

The faithful of Old died without receiving the promise, but you've inherited true riches and abundant life in Jesus Christ. God's going to complete what He started in you, *but you have to obey the laws of the kingdom.* You have to *abide* in the One who cut the new covenant that will last throughout eternity. Give everything to Jesus today. Bow your heart to Him and do whatever He tells you to do from this day forward. *Seek ye first* the kingdom of God, and everything you need will be provided.

Let's pray. "Lord Jesus, I ask that You'll continue to bring us into the full understanding of how to prosper in Your kingdom. Thank You for challenging us to prosper in our souls, so that we'll manage Your blessings with integrity and accountability. Help us to obey Your commands like Joshua obeyed the Father and to magnify You in every situation. Give us strategic wisdom that will cause us to possess everything You've destined for us to acquire. And when we come into our full inheritance, help us to help others and to seek Your kingdom first. Lord, give us *soul dominion* according to God's original plan. Help us to prosper and be in health, *even as* our souls prosper. Amen."

9

ABUNDANT LIVING BEGINS WITH SOUL PROSPERITY

Therefore if any man be in Christ, he is a new creature: old things are passed away; behold, all things are become new (2 Cor. 5:17).

Jesus is the essence of soul prosperity, the complete snapshot of everything God is to man—the second Adam—the one who *completed* the path of soul dominion. During His ministry on earth Jesus demonstrated that He could reference God on every dimension: past, present, and future. He existed in eternity and was born into the earth—and His soul was perfect, timeless...and joined to the Father.

Jesus came in the form of God and took on the likeness of man. He was the shadow of God, shaped to resemble man. And His strength is made perfect in our weaknesses (see 2 Cor. 12:7–9). He is the first fruits of the Father—the perfect living soul—the life who is the light of men (see John. 1:4). He is Lord, forever worthy to be magnified.

The scribe in Mark, chapter 12, discovered it was true when he repeated the commandments Jesus had just spoken: "Hear, O Israel; The Lord our God is one Lord: And thou shalt love the Lord thy God with all thy heart, and with all thy soul, and with all thy mind, and with all thy strength" (Mark 12:29–30). A divine match (representing number 2) was created on the spot—but it was actually the *third* time God's words had been spoken—because Jesus was quoting the Father. The number three represents resurrection, completeness, and wholeness.

The scribe got saved that day. That's why Jesus told him, "Thou art not far from the kingdom of God" (Mark 12:34). He wasn't far from receiving the promise because Jesus allowed him to see the kingdom. Remember John 3:3, "Except a man be born again, he cannot see the kingdom of God"? The scribe *saw* because he'd been saved, "If thou shalt confess with thy mouth the Lord Jesus, and shalt believe in thine heart that God hath raised him from the dead, thou shalt be saved. For with the heart man believeth unto righteousness; and with the mouth confession is made unto salvation" (Rom. 10:9–10).

And that was the difference. He could magnify the Lord and receive the promises of God. The faithful of Old could only *believe* unto righteousness (see Heb. 11:39–40), but he could *confess Jesus* and receive salvation. He was close to the kingdom because he spoke life to Life. Hebrews 11:13–14 says, "These all died in faith, not having received the promises, but having seen them afar off, and were persuaded of them, and embraced *them,* and confessed that they were strangers and pilgrims on earth. For they that say such things declare plainly that they seek a country."

On the other hand, Jesus told the Pharisees, "Yet a little while am I with you, and then I go unto him that sent me. Ye shall seek me, and shall not find me: and where I am, thither ye cannot come. If any man thirst, let him come unto me, and drink. He that believeth on me, as the scripture hath said, out of his belly shall flow rivers of living water. (But this he spake of the Spirit, which they that believe on him should receive: for the Holy Ghost was not yet given; because that Jesus was not yet glorified)" (John 7:33–34,37–39; see also Amos 8:11–13).

The Pharisees scoffed at Jesus, so they couldn't see the kingdom—*even if they sought Him.* And they definitely couldn't *enter into* the kingdom, because they rejected water and Spirit: "Except a man be born of *water* and *of* the *Spirit,* he cannot enter into the kingdom of God" (John 3:5, *emphasis mine*). The scribe, however, would inherit the promises...and *old things* would *pass away.*

The Breath of Life

Adam was given the breath of life at the beginning of time (see Gen. 2:7). Jesus—the way, the truth, and the life—"gave up the ghost" when He died on the cross and said, "Father, into thy hands I commend my spirit" (Luke 23:46). So the Holy Spirit is the "breath" of "Life," or the breath of Jesus Christ: Because John 1:5–8 says, "And the light shineth in darkness; and the darkness comprehended it not. There was a man sent from God, whose name was John. The same came for a witness, to bear witness of the Light, that all men through him might believe. He was not that Light, but was sent to bear witness of that Light."

Before He was crucified, Jesus told His disciples, "But the Comforter, which is the Holy Ghost, whom the Father will send in my name, he shall teach you all things, and bring all things to your remembrance, whatsoever I have said to you" (John 14:26). Like John, the Holy Spirit would return and bear witness of the Light. "Even the Spirit of truth; whom the world cannot receive, because it seeth him not, neither knoweth him: but ye know him; for he dwelleth with you, and shall be in you" (John 14:17).

The Holy Spirit magnifies the Lord Jesus Christ. And if we're filled with the Spirit, we can *magnify*. That's how prosperity was birthed in Adam. That's how it came back to earth through the second Adam—and that's how we enter into a corporate anointing and true wealth.

Let me explain from a different perspective. When Adam lost his inheritance, the Lord God told him, "In the sweat of thy face shalt thou eat bread, till thou return unto the ground; for out of it wast thou taken: for dust thou art, and unto dust shalt thou return" (Gen. 3:19). Adam was unfaithful in his earthly dominion, so he lost the *breath of life*...he lost the Comforter. Jesus prospered in His soul and restored our eternal inheritance.

Luke 16:10–12 [*inserts mine*] says, "He that is faithful in that which is least [earthly riches] is faithful also in much [spiritual abundance]....If therefore ye have not been faithful in the unrighteous mammon, who will commit to your trust the true riches? And if ye have not been faithful in that which is another man's, who shall give you that which is your own?"

With this in mind, Jesus told the Pharisees, "If any man thirst," to fulfill a prophetic pattern. In the Greek, *thirst* just means "thirst."[1] But in the Hebrew, the root of *thirst* means to "suffer."[2] So let me repeat what Jesus said to the Pharisees like this: "If any man is *suffering* without the Comforter, receive Me into your heart and you'll receive the *breath of life.* You'll recover the dominion Adam lost when Life left his soul. If you come to Me, you can become a *living soul* again and enter My rest."

How does John the Baptist fit in? Get ready to go deeper in the prophetic mystery. John's soul magnified the Lord and announced the kingdom of Jesus Christ for a reason. And it started in the beginning.

A New Day, a New Praise

Let's go to Psalm 34:1–3. "I will bless the Lord at all times: his praise shall continually be in my mouth. My soul shall make her boast in the Lord: the humble shall hear thereof, and be glad. O magnify the Lord with me, and let us exalt his name together." King David wrote this psalm, but he didn't inherit the promises. He magnified the Lord *by faith,* knowing he'd inherit them in the future. Now hear me. "Continually" (Ps. 34:1) and "whatsoever" (Ps. 1:3) *work together.* In other words, when *whatsoever* you do prospers in God, you've entered into *continual* praise.

On the other hand, when you lose your praise, it reveals that your soul has lost its relationship with God—just like Adam did. Let me explain. Your soul is always checking out what God's doing in the spirit realm because it was created to seek Him. When you sleep, your spirit is still communicating with God about what you've taken to Him in prayer. It even wakes you up at night because it already knows things that you can't see...*yet.*

Your mind can't understand why your soul wants to make her boast in the Lord. Your soul understands the *pruning.* Notice that David said, *My soul shall make her boast in the Lord.* Why did he use the feminine gender? In the spirit realm, your soul is connected with the womb, the part of you that gives birth and multiplies. Your soul possesses the land. You see, *natural* women always know when they're pregnant. So your soul knows supernaturally when God has put something in it that's going to be birthed.

Now let's get real. Sometimes your "belly" can feel sick because you're going through growing pains. In the spirit, this means your spirit is trying to get rid of old (dead) things in your soul. God is purging you, getting things out that can't be there on the next level. So you wake up with morning sickness, dizziness, and depression...not realizing that pain is part of the *pruning* process.

Why are the humble glad? Why do they have joy? The *pruning* produces much fruit...and it yields abundant prosperity. This is why few today truly celebrate God. Even fewer understand the significance of 1 Peter 5:6: "Humble yourselves therefore under the mighty hand of God, that he may exalt you in due time." When you get down low enough and can still declare, "Nothing's going to stop me from getting in position to know my God," you can celebrate *in everything* because your soul's already prospering in God. Your soul has the joy of the Lord.

Now I rejoice when I'm humbled—because I know God's going to do something supernatural when I get up! I might be bound, but it's only teaching me how high I'm going to rise up. *Get this into your spirit.* Second Corinthians 4:8–10 says, "*We are* troubled on every side, yet not distressed; *we are* perplexed, but not in despair; persecuted, but not forsaken; cast down, but not destroyed; always bearing about in the body the dying [*cutting*] of the Lord Jesus, that the life also of Jesus might be made manifest in our body" (*insert and emphasis mine*).

Sometimes the Lord humbles your soul so that He can add somebody to your praise—because on the next level, you're going to need a praise partner. You need the humbling: you need the *pruning* so that you can bear more spiritual fruit. You can't care about a title, who likes you, or anything else. You have to be humbled to enter the *continual* praise in Psalm 34:1.

A Supernatural Delivery

God's getting ready to take you up! Go with me to Luke 1:30–34.

And the angel said unto her, Fear not, Mary: for thou hast found favour with God.

And, behold, thou shalt conceive in thy womb, and bring forth a son, and shalt call his name JESUS.

He shall be great, and shall be called the Son of the Highest: and the Lord God shall give unto him the throne of his father David:

And he shall reign over the house of Jacob for ever; and of his kingdom there shall be no end.

Then said Mary unto the angel, How shall this be, seeing I know not a man?

This confirms it. Your mind can't handle it when your soul declares what God is doing. It will wonder, "How can this be, seeing that I don't have the right education? How can this be, when I only make this much a month? How can this be, when I've always been labeled this or that?" Here's how: "And the angel answered and said unto her, The Holy Ghost shall come upon thee, and the power of the Highest shall overshadow thee" (vs. 35).

There's a powerful mystery hidden in this passage. Let's continue. "Therefore also that holy thing which shall be born of thee shall be called the Son of God. And, behold, thy cousin Elisabeth, she hath also conceived a son" (vs. 35–36). In other words, when God sets you into the birthing process, He's already provided someone who's been humbled to accept your delivery! *You won't be out there alone.* And this person won't think you're crazy when your soul cries out and magnifies the Lord. This person is pregnant with like purpose and is also birthing out another level.

Now let's go back to verse 36. "And, behold, thy cousin Elisabeth, she hath also conceived a son in her old age: and this is the sixth month with her, who was called barren." *What does this mean?* You could be like Elisabeth and conceive in your old age—past the time you think something should have happened. We will all be perfected *in* Christ *together.*

Here are two prophetic principles: First, Scripture identified that Elisabeth was supposed to be out of season. Second, it also identified that she'd already conquered six months. According to the prophetic code, six is the number of man. So this means she'd already come past the opinions of men concerning her pregnancy. The baby's not hidden anymore; it's visible. Her over-shadowing was complete. And though others said Elisabeth was barren, she was carrying a child with supernatural power.

Many times the work of God in your life is so supernatural, it has to wait until it's past your time to do it. It's going to go past your goal and agenda spread sheet. Nevertheless, it will be done!

For with God nothing shall be impossible.

And Mary said, Behold the handmaid of the Lord; be it unto me according to thy word. And the angel departed from her.

And Mary arose in those days, and went in to the hill country with haste into a city of Juda;

And entered into the house of Zacharias, and saluted Elisabeth.

And it came to pass, that, when Elisabeth heard the salutation of Mary, the babe leaped in her womb; and Elisabeth was filled with the Holy Ghost (Luke 1:37–41).

Let me recap. Mary didn't hesitate and neither can you. When the Word impregnates your spirit, don't wait around endlessly for other people to confirm it. Mary *went with haste.* She didn't go ask her sister, "Did you see the angel? Did you feel something in the room with me? Do you sense that was the right word?"

Mary *went* and the statement Jesus would speak in the future came to pass in John: "Verily, verily, I say unto thee, Except a man be born of water and of the Spirit, he cannot enter into the kingdom of God" (John 3:5).

Here's why. John was born "of *water*" in his mother's womb, and "of the *Spirit*" through hearing Mary's salutation—*because Mary had prospered in her soul.* When her salutation came forth, it changed the atmosphere because it echoed the voice of God. And everything came under the subjection of her soul dominion.

> *And she [Elisabeth] spake out with a loud voice, and said, Blessed art thou among women, and blessed is the fruit of thy womb.*
>
> *And whence is this to me, that the mother of my Lord should come to me?*
>
> *For, lo, as soon as the voice of thy salutation sounded in mine ears, the babe leaped in my womb for joy.*
>
> *And blessed is she that believed: for there shall be a performance of those things which were told her from the Lord* (Luke 1:42–45).

Do you get this? When you're baptized in water *and* Spirit, the Word He's declared over your life will come to completion. Things will start to happen if you just magnify Him—*bless Him at all times.*

A Divine Performance

If you respond to God like Mary did, a performance will take place in your life. Declare it right now, "I can't be quiet. I've got to praise Him because He's performing something...He's doing something I couldn't measure, speak, or analyze."

And God will say, "Eyes haven't seen, ears haven't heard, neither has it entered into the heart of man what I'm about to perform in your life."

Don't get mad when people can't see what God's doing inside of you—because one day your birthing will come. Keep praising God until the atmosphere changes and something breaks loose around you! Celebrate God until something leaps for joy, inside *and* out. Keep blessing Him because your voice sets the "performance" of God's vision into motion. You have been ordained for this. And you'll receive a divine response to your declaration of faith.

That's why you have to keep checking yourself against Psalm 1: You don't walk "in the counsel of the ungodly." You don't stand "in the way of sinners." You don't sit "in the seat of the scornful" (vs. 1–3). You delight in your God, because *rivers of living water* are flowing inside of you. So rejoice in the "overshadowing," because something new is being worked in you.

This is why not just anyone can *magnify*: your soul must prosper before anything else can. Look at Luke 1:46–47: "And Mary said, My soul doth magnify the Lord, and my spirit hath rejoiced in God my Saviour." This goes beyond being traditional and typical in your praise. To "magnify" the Lord, you must have the substance *within you* that identifies with God—because you've endured the *overshadowing*.

Now let me say it this way. Not just anyone can be filled with the Holy Spirit and be baptized with joy. God has to qualify you first—because it's so supernatural, your flesh can't access or release it. To be filled with the Holy Spirit, you have to know Jesus as Lord, and surrender to Him: body, soul, and spirit.

This takes me back to the parable of the talents. The owner gave five talents to one servant, to another two, and to another one. The servants with five and two talents traded them and yielded a return. To each of them he said, "Well done, thou good and faithful servant: thou hast been faithful over a few things, I will make thee ruler over many things: enter thou into the joy of thy lord" (Mat. 25:21,23). They were qualified for joy *before* they received it.

The problem we face is that we're trying to "get the joy" without doing anything for God. "Oh, I'm just going to church to get joy today." Then all you're seeking is hype—not the kingdom. "Oh, that was a good service. I just love the Lord because it felt good today." That's hype. *Listen.* Elisabeth had to carry her baby for six months before she got a taste of joy! If you're going to possess joy, you have to be qualified for it.

Here's a prophetic principle: Real joy carries you through the last three months of your birthing! It strengthens you to carry the weight of the burden God has placed upon you. Joy equipped Jesus to endure the cross (see Heb. 12:2); *especially during the overshadowing period between the sixth and ninth* hours, when He finally gave up the ghost. Let's examine the numbers: Man (representing number 6) was reborn (representing number 9), and 9 minus 6 equals 3, representing resurrection, completion, and wholeness. It was finished!

The Process to Perfection

When Elisabeth was filled with the Holy Spirit, she was perfected in Christ. And her son, John the Baptist, testified of Him. The second manifestation came when he baptized Jesus in the Jordan River. "And Jesus, when he was baptized, went up straightway out of the water: and, lo, the heavens were opened unto him, and he saw the Spirit of God descending like a dove, and lighting upon him: And lo a voice from heaven, saying, This is my beloved Son, in whom I am well pleased" (Matt. 3:16–17). Water and Spirit: *Divine agreement.*

This takes me back to John 3:3–5. In verse 3, *seeing the kingdom* represents old covenant believers; and in verse 5, *entering into the kingdom* represents new covenant believers. Old covenant believers could see through the prophets, but they couldn't *enter in* because Christ their Messiah had not been given. But when He was conceived in Mary's womb, a divine opportunity came back to life.

Here's another prophetic principle: God parted two bodies of water to bring the nation of Israel into abundant life: the Red Sea and the Jordan River. The first body of water delivered them from bondage, and the second body brought a divine release of prosperity. What does this say to you? Has your soul prospered?

Have you come out of bondage? Then your season of prosperity in God is coming!

Mary and Elisabeth carried the prophetic seed of Abraham to fruition. God cut the covenant with Abraham when he was ninety-nine years old. Let's examine this number again: Mary gave birth (representing number 9) to Jesus, who would deliver all nations from bondage; and Elisabeth gave birth (representing number 9) to John the Baptist, who symbolized the Holy Spirit—the One who'd perform every divine promise.

Is your soul leaping for joy? Then let's go to Acts 2:1-4. "And when the day of Pentecost was fully come, they were all with one accord in one place. And suddenly there came a sound from heaven as of a rushing mighty wind, and it filled all the house where they were sitting. And there appeared unto them cloven tongues like as of fire, and it sat upon each of them. And they were all filled with the Holy Ghost, and began to speak with other tongues, as the Spirit gave them utterance." Let's look at this from the prophetic perspective.

Mary was overshadowed in conception and filled with the Holy Spirit. Some time passed, and she visited Elisabeth…then water and Spirit birthed the joy of the Lord. Later, Jesus was overshadowed on the cross. Three days passed and He ascended to heaven. So when the Comforter came on the day of Pentecost—it fulfilled a three-part pattern! The prophetic process was complete: because Jesus had already declared, "The wind bloweth where it listeth, and thou hearest the sound thereof, but canst not tell whence it cometh, and whither it goeth: so is everyone that is born of the Spirit" (John 3:8).

Now let's look at another angle. Four hundred years passed between the old and new covenants. So there was a passing of time between when God gave the promises, and when Jesus fulfilled them. Are *you seeing the pattern?*

The bottom line is, *God is perfecting His church.* And the *infilling* of the Holy Spirit is *vital* because that's how you're able to walk out God's purpose in the earth. That's why Jesus, the living Word, is "quick, and powerful, and sharper than any twoedged sword, piercing even to the dividing asunder of soul and spirit, and of the joints and marrow, and is a discerner of the thoughts and intents of the heart" (Heb. 4:12). *Now read carefully.*

God *cut* into flesh to create a new covenant. Later, God *cut* a covenant with Abraham and called him the "father of many nations," who would inherit the Promised Land (see Gen. 17:1–8). Much later, in light of Hebrews 4:12 and our knowledge today that Jesus is the Word and has living water to give, we can see that God cut into human flesh and divided joint and marrow in the *living waters* of Mary's womb. And she gave birth to Jesus in a stable (Luke 2:7), which means blood and water hit the ground that had been cursed after Adam's fall. Later still, after Jesus died, a soldier pierced His side (*cut* His flesh) and blood and water flowed again (John 19:34). The third part of the pattern was fulfilled, which brought resurrection, completion, and wholeness...for eternity.

Let me say it plainly. The baptism of the Holy Spirit completes your salvation and seals your divine inheritance, because without it, *you can't magnify God.* You can't worship Him in Spirit and in Truth. You can't please Him and fulfill the *Torah* of the Soul. *Human flesh has to be cut.* Let me wrap it all up with 2 Peter 1:2–10.

> *Grace and peace be multiplied unto you through the knowledge of God, and of Jesus our Lord,*
>
> *According as his divine power hath given unto us all things that pertain unto life and godliness...*
>
> *Whereby are given unto us exceeding great and precious promises: that by these ye might be partakers of the divine nature...*
>
> *And beside this, giving all diligence, add to your faith virtue; and to virtue knowledge;*
>
> *And to knowledge temperance; and to temperance patience; and to patience godliness;*
>
> *And to godliness brotherly kindness; and to brotherly kindness charity.*
>
> *For if these things be in you, and abound, they make you that ye shall neither be barren nor unfruitful in the knowledge of our Lord Jesus Christ.*
>
> *But he that lacketh these things is blind, and cannot see afar off, and hath forgotten that he was purged from his old sins.*
>
> *Wherefore the rather, brethren, give diligence to make your calling and election sure: for if ye do these things, ye shall never fall.*

Jesus—*the living Word*—is discerning your heart right now, because the Spirit of God can pierce through the heart of your soul. Have you been filled with the Holy Spirit? If so, you can worship God in (Holy) Spirit and in Truth (Jesus Christ). Jesus can save you *to the uttermost.* Adam lost the *eternal* part of his soul as part of the curse. But Jesus came, completed the divine process, and sent the Holy Spirit back to earth. Then the Holy Spirit reconnected the eternal heart of God with the mortal heart of man, which is why you can govern your soul through the power of the Holy Spirit. You can have soul dominion.

Jesus enters your soul through the heart of God (who is a Spirit) within you and releases divine prosperity into the natural realm...so blessings come from the inside out. And you can be a witness unto Him (see Acts 1:8) because, through the Holy Spirit, God has performed the same work in you that He did in Adam. And as He speaks into your soul through the doorway of your heart, you must declare what you hear to create a divine match and see His kingdom come in the earth.

If you're not filled with the Spirit, God can be *with* you—but He can't be *in* you...and you need Him *within* for your soul to prosper. That's why David said in Psalm 51:10,12, "Create in me a clean heart, O God; and renew a right spirit within me. Restore unto me the joy of thy salvation; and uphold me with thy free spirit." Create...renew... restore. From Old, to New, to Perfected: This is the prophetic pattern of soul dominion.

O Magnify the Lord With Me

Let's make room for Jesus in the heart of our souls...*and magnify Him together.* Satan attacked the corporate anointing bestowed upon Adam and Eve, and they lost their inheritance. *He divided them and conquered.* He slithered over to Eve and asked, "Yea, hath God said?" Something vital was missing, and here it is: *The enemy knew God, but not as Lord,* so he couldn't even say the Word. Don't let the enemy steal your praise. Let's magnify the Lord together!

Here's a final prophetic pattern, which is illustrated on the following pages. Moses' Tabernacle in the wilderness is where Israel gathered as a nation before God. It was their place of unity, and the place where God spoke. There were three levels: the Outer Court, the Holy Place, and the Most Holy Place. Now humor me while I illustrate.

This is how it plays out. You're standing with others in the Outer Court, having just come into the knowledge of Christ as Lord—lifting up praises to God.

God causes you to start magnifying His Lordship by teaching you to worship Him in Spirit and in Truth. You begin to move closer to Him.

Another person begins to draw closer to God, and you touch in agreement for her to begin magnifying as you had done—and God draws you deeper inside of the Holy Place. You magnify Him even more and begin to prosper your soul.

Everyone begins to unite in corporate agreement and the prophetic cycle intensifies. She moves up to the Holy Place; and when you touch and agree with her on *this* level, God draws you into the Holy of Holies. You begin to love Him with all of your heart, soul, mind, and strength…and you love your neighbor as yourself. You praise, exalt, and magnify His name as He fills you with His power and glory—your soul arises in the abundance of divine prosperity.

Everyone magnifies the Lord together and celebrates with those who've been blessed to go before them. God perfects you as you magnify Him, and you possess your eternal inheritance in God as He releases you into the fullness of His kingdom. You arise declaring His words in completed soul dominion. And *whatsoever* you do is blessed, *even as your soul prospers.*

What's the prophetic principle? Everybody who's seeking the kingdom of God will embrace the corporate anointing. And they'll keep praising God until their turn comes up. *Magnify*...with me! Every person rejoices when somebody else gets promoted. *Magnify*...with me! Everyone shares the wealth God has given them. *Magnify*...with me! Everyone enters the eternal kingdom. *Magnify*...with me! And everyone inherits the promises...*together.*

Choose Ye This Day...

This is true prosperity. This is soul dominion. It's also why God *expects* our souls to prosper. "But Christ as a son over His own house; whose house are we, if we hold fast the confidence and the rejoicing of the hope firm unto the end. Take heed, brethren, lest there be in any of you an evil heart of unbelief, in departing from the living God. But exhort one another daily, while it is called To day; lest any of you be hardened through the deceitfulness of sin. For we are made partakers of Christ, if we hold the beginning of our confidence steadfast to the end" (Heb. 3:6,12–14).

Lay aside every weight, and run patiently on the path the Lord sets before you; because it leads to supernatural wealth and abundance! Keep looking to Jesus, the author and finisher of our faith, who endured the cross, and ascended to the throne room of God (see Heb. 12:1–2). Choose *this day* the real path to abundance, and God won't forget your labors of love. Choose soul prosperity, and *exceeding abundant* blessings will be added to you. Choose soul dominion, and everything that God bestowed upon Adam (in the beginning)...*will be yours.*

Let's bow our heads in a final prayer. "God, we thank You for Your presence. Now bring us into a place of illumination and fill us with supernatural strength and understanding from Your throne. Give us heavenly wisdom through the mind of Christ. And give us lips of clay that can be purged, so that we'll declare Your Word in truth—knowing it won't return to You void. Give us the Holy Spirit to manifest the mighty works You've begun in heaven that will be fulfilled in the earth. Thank You for taking us to another level in You. Lord, give us the keys to a new mansion that's closer to Your throne and deeper in Your love. Speak the Truth into our souls by the power of the Holy Spirit, and we'll walk in Your *soul dominion.* Lord, we thank You that it's already done in Jesus' name, Amen."

Endnotes

Introduction

[1] Rabbi Nosson Scherman, *The Chumash*, The ArtScroll Series®/Stone Edition (Brooklyn, NY: Mesorah Publications, Ltd., 1998, 2000), p. 2.

[2] Rami Danieli, meeting with the editor, 8 Aug. 2002.

Chapter 1

[1] James Strong, *The New Strong's Complete Dictionary of Bible Words* (Nashville: Thomas Nelson Publishers, 1996), "English Word Index," s.v. "dust," entry 6083, p. 81; defined "Hebrew/Aramaic Dictionary," entries 6080, 6083, pp. 479-480.

[2] ibid., *Index,* s.v. "image," pp. 133-134, entry 6754 *Hebrew/Aramaic,* p. 500; s.v. "likeness," p. 154, entry 1823 *Hebrew/Aramaic,* p. 348.

[3] ibid., *English,* s.v. "breathed," p. 34, entry 5301 *Hebrew/Aramaic,* p. 456.

[4] ibid., English, s.v. "breath," p. 34, entry 5397 *Hebrew/Aramaic,* p. 459.

[5] Sol Steinmetz, Editor-in-Chief, *Webster's American Family Dictionary* (New York, NY: Random House, Inc., 1998), p. 867.

[6] Juanita Bynum, Ph.D., *Matters of the Heart* (Lake Mary, FL: Charisma House, 2002), pp. 106 and 102.

[7] Scherman, *The Chumash,* p. 27.

[8] Steinmetz, p. 677.

[9] Genesis 17:5 tells us that God changed Abram's name to "Abraham": "Neither shall thy name any more be called Abram, but thy name shall be Abraham; for a father of many nations have I made thee."

Chapter 2

[1] Steinmetz, p. 695.

Chapter 3

[1] Strong, *English*, s.v. "vagabond," in Acts 19:13, p. 269, entry 4022 "Greek Dictionary," p. 679.

[2] ibid., *English*, s.v. "power," in Acts 1:8, p. 197, entry 1411 *Greek*, p. 606.

Chapter 5

[1] AMP, "Deuteronomion," p. 211.

Chapter 6

[1] Strong, *English*, s.v. "pricks," p. 200, entry 2759 *Greek*, p. 645.

Chapter 9

[1] ibid., *English*, s.v. "thirst," p. 257, entries 1372, 1373 *Greek*, p. 605.

[2] ibid., entries 6772 and 6770.

Recommended Reading

365 Ways To Become A Millionaire (Without Being Born One), Brain Koslow, The Penguin Group, Copyright © 1999.

The Achiever's Guide To Success, Dr. E. Bernard Jordan, Zoe Ministries, Copyright © 1996 (second printing).

The Instant Millionaire (A Tale of Wisdom and Wealth), Mark Fisher, New World Library, Copyright © 1990.

The Power of Money, Dr. E. Bernard Jordan, Zoe Ministries, Copyright © 1992.

Prayer of Salvation

God loves you—no matter who you are, no matter what your past. God loves you so much that He gave His one and only begotten Son for you. The Bible tells us that "...whoever believes in him shall not perish but have eternal life" (John 3:16 NIV). Jesus laid down His life and rose again so that we could spend eternity with Him in heaven and experience His absolute best on earth. If you would like to receive Jesus into your life, say the following prayer out loud and mean it from your heart.

Heavenly Father, I come to You admitting that I am a sinner. Right now, I choose to turn away from sin, and I ask You to cleanse me of all unrighteousness. I believe that Your Son, Jesus, died on the cross to take away my sins. I also believe that He rose again from the dead so that I might be forgiven of my sins and made righteous through faith in Him. I call upon the name of Jesus Christ to be the Savior and Lord of my life. Jesus, I choose to follow You and ask that You fill me with the power of the Holy Spirit. I declare that right now I am a child of God. I am free from sin and full of the right-eousness of God. I am saved in Jesus' name. Amen.

If you prayed this prayer to receive Jesus Christ as your Savior for the first time, please contact us on the Web at **www.harrisonhouse.com** to receive a free book.

Or you may write to us at:

Harrison House
P.O. Box 35035
Tulsa, Oklahoma 74153

About the Author

Thomas Weeks, III is a bishop, prophet, conference host, and highly sought after motivational speaker. He is Co-founder and Bishop of the Global Destiny Christian Community along with his wife, Senior Pastor Dr. Juanita Bynum Weeks, headquartered in the Washington D.C. metropolitan area.

A socially concerned entrepreneur and educator, Bishop Weeks has spearheaded several community service organizations, the Internet's *Destiny Network,* and is also establishing Destiny University. Bishop Weeks studied Mass Communications at the University of Delaware, holds a Bachelor of Arts degree in Theology, and is pursuing advanced studies toward a Master of Arts in Christian Counseling at the Christian International College of Theology.

MINISTRY INFORMATION

Bishop Thomas Weeks, III

P.O. Box 60866

Washington, DC 20039

Executive Office:

Ministry Office: 202-829-4151

Facsimile: 202-829-4153

e-mail: Info@MyGlobalDestiny.com

Website: www.MyGlobalDestiny.com

Visit Bishop Thomas Weeks, III
at www.MyGlobalDestiny.com

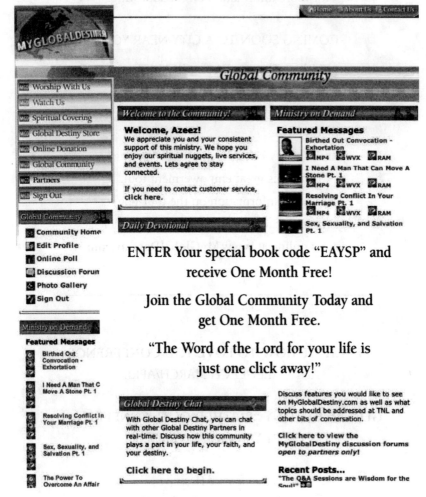

Visit www.MYGLOBALDESTINY.COM
for more information on the following:

COMING SOON TO A CITY NEAR YOU:

Bishop Thomas Weeks, III Ministries
Presents – "Mystery of Love"
Global World Tour 2005

Join Bishop Weeks, III as he tours the nation
with this great empowerment tour.
For more information on the tour guide,
registration or to order your conference package
visit us online at **www.MyGlobalDestiny.com**

TEACH ME HOW TO LOVE YOU CONFERENCE
ANNUALLY EACH MARCH/APRIL

GLOBAL DESTINY "BIRTHED OUT" CONFERENCE
EVERY YEAR IN NOVEMBER

Conference Hosts:
**Bishop Thomas Weeks, III
and Dr. Juanita Bynum Weeks**

For registration and more information visit us online at
www.MyGlobalDestiny.com

OTHER BOOKS BY BISHOP THOMAS WEEKS, III

The Book *Teach Me How To Love You* with bonus CD

COMING SOON:
- ❖ TEACH ME HOW TO LOVE YOU - THE DEVOTIONAL
- ❖ TEACH ME HOW TO LOVE YOU - THE FIRST YEAR
- ❖ SUCCESS BEGINS WITH A SYSTEM

www.harrisonhouse.com

Fast. Easy. Convenient!

- ◆ New Book Information
- ◆ Look Inside the Book
- ◆ Press Releases
- ◆ Bestsellers

- ◆ Free E-News
- ◆ Author Biographies
- ◆ Upcoming Books
- ◆ Share Your Testimony

For the latest in book news and author information, please visit us on the Web at www.harrisonhouse.com. Get up-to-date pictures and details on all our powerful and life-changing products. Sign up for our e-mail newsletter, *Friends of the House,* and receive free monthly information on our authors and products including testimonials, author announcements, and more!

Harrison House—
Books That Bring Hope, Books That Bring Change

The Harrison House Vision

Proclaiming the truth and the power
Of the Gospel of Jesus Christ
With excellence;

Challenging Christians to
Live victoriously,
Grow spiritually,
Know God intimately.